011565

784.409
MYR   Myrus, Donald
       Ballads, blues, and the
       big beat

Date Due

JAN 18			
MAR 2 0			
JAN			

An American art form is explored from
the point of view of its creators and performers, as well as the fans who popularize it.
Traditional and latest aspects of this field are
covered.

BALLADS, BLUES, and the BIG BEAT

Books by Donald Myrus

KEEPING UP WITH THE ASTRONAUTS

COLLECTORS' GUNS

STORY IN THE SAND
(With Albert Squillace)

I LIKE JAZZ

A MAN'S WORK

BALLADS, BLUES, AND THE BIG BEAT

BALLADS,
BLUES,
and the
BIG BEAT

by Donald Myrus

The Macmillan Company

Collier-Macmillan Limited, London

To Ellen Count

The Macmillan Company, New York
866 Third Avenue, New York, New York 10022
Collier-Macmillan Canada, Ltd., Toronto, Ontario
Library of Congress catalog card number: 66-16104
Printed in the United States of America

THIRD PRINTING, 1969

*Permission to quote from copyrighted material is
gratefully acknowledged to the following:*

Appleseed Music, Inc. for *Talking Cuban Crisis* and *Talking Vietnam* by Phil Ochs
(both © Copyright 1963 by Appleseed Music, Inc.) and *There but for Fortune* by Phil Ochs
(© Copyright 1963, 1964 by Appleseed Music, Inc.). Bibo Music Publishers, Inc. for
Old Man Atom by Vern Partlow. *Broadside* Magazine, 215 W. 98 St., New York, N.Y. 10025 for
excerpts by Phil Ochs and Patrick Sky from *Broadside #54*. Cherry Lane Music, Inc.
for *The Willing Conscript (I've Never Killed Before)*, words and music by Tom Paxton (© 1963
Cherry Lane Music, Inc.) and *What Did You Learn in School Today?*, words and music
by Tom Paxton (© 1962 Teena Music Corp.). E. P. Dutton & Co., Inc. for BOUND FOR GLORY
by Woody Guthrie. Folkways Records, Inc. for BOUND FOR GLORY jacket notes by
Millard Lampell; the will of Joe Hill from REBEL VOICES; OLD TIME MUSIC AT CLARENCE
ASHLEY'S, edited and annotated by Ralph and Richard Rinzler; and excerpts from the
September 1965 issue of *Sing Out!* Harcourt, Brace & World, Inc. and Brandt & Brandt for
Inside the Whale from SUCH, SUCH WERE THE JOYS by George Orwell. Horizon Press, Inc.
and Cassell & Co., Ltd. for the foreword by Richard Wright to BLUES FELL IN THE
MORNING by Paul Oliver. Leeds Music Corp. for *Joe Hill*, music by Earl Robinson, words
by Alfred Hayes (© Copyright MCMXXXVIII by MCA Music a division of MCA Inc., New York,
Leeds Music Co.). *The New York Times* for a review by Robert Shelton (© 1961 by The New
York Times Company). Oak Publications for *Leadbelly* by Pete Seeger and excerpts by
Woody Guthrie, both from LEADBELLY SONGBOOK; and THE POETRY OF THE BLUES by
Samuel Charters. *Pageant Magazine* for excerpts from the March 1964 issue. Peer International
Corp. for *Worried Man Blues* by A. P. Carter. Schroder Music Company for *Little Boxes*
and *What Have They Done to the Rain?*, words and music by Malvina Reynolds (© Copyright
1962 by Schroder Music Co.). *Sing Out!* Magazine for an article by Phil Ochs from the
September 1965 issue; an article by Peter LaFarge from the March 1965 issue, and *Woody Guthrie—
Some Reminiscences* by Pete Seeger. Tempo Music Pub., R. J. Carew, Washington, D.C. 20011,
for "Mama, mama, take a look at Sis" from *Winin' Boy Blues* by Jelly Roll Morton.
The University of Michigan Press for REBEL VOICES: AN I.W.W. ANTHOLOGY by Joyce L.
Kornbluh (Copyright The University of Michigan). Vanguard Recording Society, Inc. for
JOAN BAEZ / 5 jacket notes by L. Hughes; THE GREENBRIAR BOYS (Vanguard Record
Album VRS 9104) jacket notes by Ralph Rinzler; and *Delta Blues* and *Dead and Gone* by
Julius Lester. The Village Voice, Inc. and Phil Ochs for an August 12, 1965, letter by Phil Ochs
in *The Village Voice*. Whitfield Music, Inc. for *Give to the Cause* by Patrick Sky (© Copyright
1964 Whitfield Music, Inc.).

Contents

I THANK *Ellen Count, Barry Feinstein,*
Bonnie Garner, Elliot Horne,
Judy Lishinsky, Michael Mason,
Joyce Myrus, Aaron Norman,
Alan Rinzler, Mary Ann Stuart—
in addition to many of the men and
women mentioned in these pages—for
insights and information.—DM

1 Who For, What For

This book is about the power and pleasure of folk songs and how they came to be so compelling. How from Selma to Berkeley, from Newport to the Big Sur, in schools and in colleges, at home and at work, folk songs have played a part in times that are really changing.

While mostly compelling to teenagers, the book's subject has proven to be of interest to all who want to know where it's at and who can't help wondering where we're bound. For precocious preteenagers to open-minded octogenarians, then, the book's only admission requirements are an ability to read and a curiosity about songs and their singers. I have assumed that regardless of your age, if you're interested in folk singing you're old enough to read a newspaper and to listen to a news broadcast. As a consequence you know there are wars going on and that not all people think war a great school for making men or the best way of ennobling a nation; and that patriotism doesn't mean the same thing to everybody. You also know that strikes occur and that labor unions have a great heritage if not a promising future. Folk songs cover these topics and others that come to grips with the facts of life. Listening to them is a good way to broaden your education, and education, that's the thing. Right?

Some of the songs this book is about radically challenge the cherished beliefs of earlier generations, some praise heroes who never should be forgotten, some help put the sentiment in romance, and some, the spice in lovemaking. Moreover, many of the newer songs involve situations familiar to the increasing number of people who live in cities and suburbs and not, as in the past, to farm people, who are dwindling in number.

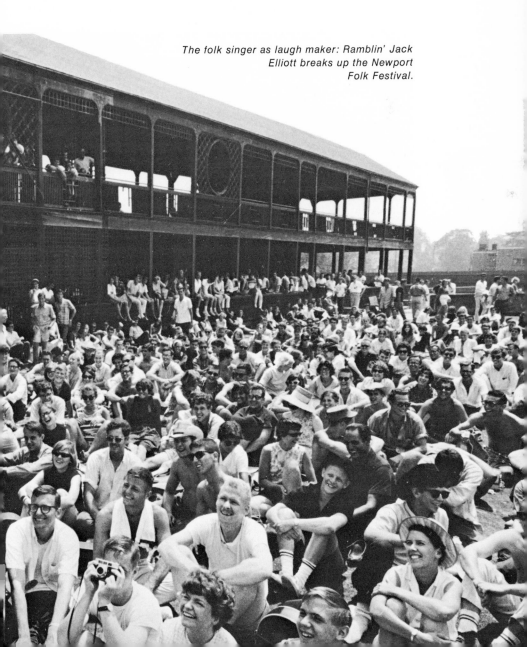

The folk singer as laugh maker: Ramblin' Jack Elliott breaks up the Newport Folk Festival.

For folk songs, words are more important than the beat—except not always. Not, for example, with blues created by Negroes, in which the rhythm pattern is always important while the words are often unintelligible to ears of whites or Negroes of middle-class upbringing. More and more, too, folk songs are written in a rock 'n' roll style.

(From in front, so there will be no misunderstanding, I think rock 'n' roll is *marvelous*; not all of it, of course, but the best of it.)

Generally, the folk sound is kept simple, and for that reason tunes usually are played on the guitar (the unamplified kind), the banjo, which has been discovered to be just right for picking at blazing speed, and on the mandolin, the fiddle, the recorder, the harmonica, the mouth bow, the dobro, the dulcimer, and assorted other instrument oddities. Folk songs generally are not backed up by piano, drums, horns, and reeds—the main instruments of jazz. Once again there are exceptions: rock 'n' roll needs partial jazz instrumentation while rockabilly and folk-rock couldn't get along without the electrified guitar.

Folk singer—a more or less arbitrary classification—is used to describe a multitude of types. Labels come easy but they don't stay fixed. Some folk singers, for example, deny that's what they are, while others who claim the title might better pick another, any other—vaudeville entertainer might be more accurate. But it's a term we're stuck with for the simple reason that everyone uses it, no matter how loosely.

To achieve some clarity in these pages there is consequently much discussion of singers of protest songs, of hillbilly weepers, of old-time ballads and blues, but little about musical-comedy numbers. Rock 'n' roll singers, such as the Supremes, are touched upon, but straight pop singers, such as Dean Martin, are not. Outside of a mention, now and then, of the Beatles, the book is limited to American singers and mostly American songs. Thus, the British singer Ewan MacColl — whom some consider the folk singer's folk singer—is passed by, and so are the folk songs, both traditional and modern, of foreign countries. Even some American singers are left out; only those I think the most important or the most interesting are presented.

(Although mostly singers are discussed it is important to note that many who achieve wide acceptance do so because of the support they get from virtuosos such as guitar players Dick Rosmini and Mike Bloomfield, and bass players Herb Brown and Bob Mathews.)

In a sense, it is a fan book: an appreciation of professionals, most of whom make their living singing to others for many reasons, not the least of which is money. Some of the professionals it touches upon go back to the turn of the century, when reward for a night of lively singing and playing was more likely to be a chicken supper or a jug of whiskey than hard cash. However, most of the book is devoted to singers active since the fifties: to those who have made records and have appeared on radio and television, and in nightclubs and coffeehouses.

Birchers and Minutemen and Stuffed Shirts: beware! If you think Pete Seeger a subversive, or brave, sweet-voiced Joan Baez a misguided fool, then this book is apt to shake you up.

If, on the other hand, you are not uptight and if you like the work of Bob Dylan and would like to have him and his disciples related to the old masters Woody Guthrie and Leadbelly, then this is your *bag*. You dig?

And, if you agree that Elvis is one of the prime changers of our time (after all, he revolutionized what most of us most often listen to) then here you'll be at home.

Welcome!

2 Poems, Protests, and Put Downs

Bob Dylan is a poet who, like those of old, *sings*. And, like important poets always, he stirs our imaginations. He is a storyteller and soothsayer who quickly spellbinds us by wrapping his words in fetching melodies and driving rhythms and by singing them in a fantastically weird style—crude rather than cultivated. He's also a rollicking harmonica howler, an adequate guitar picker, and an individual enough folk singer to break with tradition by adopting the big beat of rock 'n' roll.

This makes him a very unusual living poet: one with an audience of millions. We listen, perhaps we sing along, certainly we tap our feet, occasionally we even dance to one of his songs, and, if we are of a mind to, we begin to understand that a man possessed by dreams is telling us how things seem to him . . . not how he'd like them to be . . . not how he thinks we'd like them to be

. . . not how Ma or Pa or Teacher said they would be. He tells us that not much is *really* sacred, says at one point, in fact, that "all is phony"—which is just about the conclusion reached several thousand years ago by the Preacher (the son of King David of Jerusalem) who said "all is vanity."

Dylan warns us about following leaders, about doing things we don't believe in, and about accepting too easily promises that might not be fulfilled. In *Subterranean Homesick Blues,* for example, he takes a crack at the sacred idea that education will get you everywhere. Dylan, by the way, is a dropout. He went to the University of Minnesota for about six months.

But for a poet who finds that not much is sacred and who castigates our materialistic civilization with a tirade of abusive phrases he is not a pessimist. He tells us that life will go on at least and that we've got nothing *really* to fear.

Dylan's songs, his appearance, his few public statements have brought him a legion of admirers (just about all of them under thirty) who think of him as their cool champion in the war between the generations—a war in which teenagers and those in their twenties struggle against the Square World and its members who are thought of as too tense and too fearful and too selfish and, therefore, incapable of understanding the changing times.

Not an unusual sort of hassle—it has been occurring between fathers and sons since the beginning—but one that in certain periods gets meaner than in others. The nineteen-twenties was one such period. The English novelist and essayist George Orwell (1903–1950) in his essay *Inside the Whale* states:

"The fight that always occurs between the generations was exceptionally bitter at the end of the Great War . . . Owing probably to the ease and security of life in England, which even the war hardly disturbed, many people whose ideas were formed in the [eighteen] eighties or earlier had carried them quite unmodified into the nineteen-twenties. Meanwhile, so far as the younger gen-

This is a portrait of Bob Dylan, the world's most successful singing poet. Would you believe he started his career wearing a sweatshirt and a Huck Finn cap?

eration was concerned, the official beliefs were dissolving like sand-castles. The slump in religious beliefs, for instance, was spectacular. For several years the old-young antagonism took on a quality of real hatred. What was left of the war generation had crept out of the massacre to find their elders still bellowing the slogans of 1914."

In 1966 many members of another generation of elders are bellowing again about the need to wage war, as if nuclear bombs had never been dropped and the atmosphere never poisoned. Most of all, they bellow about the youngsters who the elders say don't appreciate what they have and who show no respect for them—the elders.

Many teenagers not admiring the middle-aged have found in Dylan a big brother—not too old, but old enough in their view to have really lived. As a consequence, he's imitated. Because Dylan is skinny, one young folk singer went on a diet to get the right look; and because Dylan appeared, early in his career, to have just stepped off a ranch after dipping sheep and not to have been near a barber, a comb, or a bottle of Wildroot for three months, others tried to look equally scruffy.

He is a paradoxical hero: one who seldom gives an interview (exceptions include interviews by Nat Hentoff—*The New Yorker,* October 24, 1964; *Playboy,* March, 1966—and Maura Davis, *Cavalier,* February, 1966), seldom welcomes the attention of his fans, and almost always shuns publicity about his personal life. Yet he courts notoriety; for example, he sang at the 1965 Newport Folk Festival not traditional-type folk songs but rock 'n' roll ones. (At Newport he wore a two-foot-high top hat.)

This phenomenon with a peculiar public personality ("a weird monkey," to use one of his epithets) nevertheless has the distinction of being called a genius. Some have objected to the label, I think erroneously. For a genius is, according to the poet W. H. Auden, writing in the Foreword to Dag Hammarskjöld's book

MARKINGS, ". . . a person with a single overwhelming talent and passion for some particular activity—be it poetry or physics or bird-watching—which determines, usually early in life, exactly what his function on earth is to be."

Dylan, born in 1941, grew up in Hibbing, Minnesota—a town of some eighteen thousand in the open-pit mining country in the northeastern part of the state—went to high school there and, like most kids, was raised by his parents. He has beclouded other facts about his early childhood and teens and, because he is an ingenious fellow, he has managed to bring off the difficult feat of being a star in the shadows. He is a master of obscurantism, most often employing the technique of exaggeration. When pressed by rapacious journalists or curious admirers he responds with unbounded imagination. This is not an unprecedented reaction to early-achieved stardom; Marlon Brando, for example, when he found himself surveying the world from "the top of a pile of candy" spun some pretty fantastic stories about how he got to his sugary perch. Such foolishness is, by and large, harmless and makes for good box office, but it's one good reason why we shouldn't take Dylan's accounts of his private past too seriously. What Dylan's tendency to tell tall tales does reflect is a determination to make a clean break with the influences of his family and hometown, thereby permitting him to make a new, unfettered life for himself. He's a young man who, in his teens, broke away from the apron strings.

In this connection I'm reminded of the movie *Billy Liar*. Perhaps you remember how Billy failed to break away from his family. Billy had a great talent, but it was not recognized, let alone understood, by his parents. Billy, on his day for big decisions, tried to make it on his own. He got to the railroad station, but lost his nerve. Even though encouraged by a vivacious, beautiful, free-spirited girl, he just couldn't bring himself to leave dull, conventional but safe Stradhoughton for the adventure and danger of London. Billy stayed home with Ma and Pa and his dreams of

Ambrosia. Bob Dylan struck out across the country and found his *Ambrosia* in Greenwich Village.

In 1961 readers of *The New York Times* learned of his existence from a review by Robert Shelton of a performance at Gerde's Folk City in Greenwich Village.

"Resembling a cross between a choir boy and a beatnik, Mr. Dylan has a cherubic look and a mop of tousled hair he partly covers with a Huck Finn black corduroy cap. His clothes may need a bit of tailoring, but when he works his guitar, harmonica or piano and composes new songs faster than he can remember them, there is no doubt that he is bursting at the seams with talent."

By then, Dylan already had a contract with Columbia Records. He was signed up by John Hammond, Sr., who, by the way, as long ago as the thirties helped produce the records of Billie Holiday, Count Basie and Benny Goodman.

Joan Baez shared her audience with Dylan until he was a star in his own right. Asked, by a magazine interviewer, about their association, he drolly replied, "The only thing I can tell you about Joan Baez is that she's not Belle Starr."

John Hammond signed Dylan for Columbia Records. For a while colleagues referred with ridicule to "Hammond's Folly." But hundreds of thousands of record buyers changed all that.

His first album, titled simply BOB DYLAN, was a near disaster financially. Copies could be bought at sacrifice prices. In fact, it wasn't until Joan Baez and Peter, Paul, and Mary kept telling their audiences how good he was that he began to catch on. But the performance is a whooper. Dylan bursts forth—a popping, chuckling, rhythmic dynamo with guitar driving and harmonica laughing.

In the next four years five more of his albums appeared: THE FREEWHEELIN' BOB DYLAN, THE TIMES THEY ARE A-CHANGIN', ANOTHER SIDE OF BOB DYLAN, BRINGING IT ALL BACK HOME, and HIGHWAY 61 REVISITED. The most popular of his songs recorded during this period were *Blowin' in the Wind, A Hard Rain's A-Gonna Fall, All I Really Want to Do, The Times They Are A-Changin', Don't Think Twice It's All Right, Subterranean Homesick Blues, Mr. Tambourine Man,* and *Like a Rollin' Stone.*

Several of these Dylan compositions are popular whether sung by Dylan or others, and even when performed as instrumentals. *Blowin' in the Wind,* for example, was not only a juke-box favorite in the Peter, Paul, and Mary version and a mainstay of civil-rights rallies and protest marches but also an instrumental choice of the jazz saxophonist Stan Getz and of the Muzak Company, which piped it over supermarket loudspeakers.

Dylan has been a growing, changing artist. The change can be marked from the blues and country-and-western-influenced songs he sang as a performer of promise at the Gaslight in 1961 (recorded on his first album) to the intensely personal musical poems of his later albums.

Along the way he stopped writing songs of social protest such as *With God on Our Side* and *Masters of War*. As far as *Masters of War* is concerned, any change would have been for the better. It is, in my opinion, a throwback to Populist propaganda, with its paranoid belief that wars are caused by sinister, old, profit-mongering Wall Street manipulators, the kind with bloodshot eyeballs popping and long fingers grasping at the prospect of a bag marked with a dollar sign. Phooey. Nations make wars. Almost everybody jumps in; and the hard fact is that a lot of people profit, some in money, some in excitement, and a lot lose—some their lives (young and old, rich and poor). War is bad enough without falsifying its causes. To give Dylan his due, he imagines how bad. Listen to his *A Hard Rain's A-Gonna Fall*.

The way he comes on—the outward appearance of the inner man—changed also. The change can be traced through the photographs on the jackets of his first, third, and fifth albums.

On the first album is a picture of a slightly vapid-looking boy, pink-faced, with long but clean fingernails and heavy sideburns, wearing a corduroy cap and a cotton suede coat lined with imitation fleece. He looks very funny.

By the third album, intensity has replaced vapidity. He comes on with a look that says, in the words of an anonymous *Newsweek* writer, that "He has suffered; he has been hung up, man, without bread, without a chick, with twisted wires growing inside him."

With the fifth album the evolution is complete—from country

boy to city kook, from sweat-shirted cherub to cuff-linked bo-
hemian. For this album there is a girl (there was one on the
second album, too: loving, smiling, possessing)—a chick who is
"high classed" (to use Elvis' term) and who is cool with not a
trace of a twinkle. There is a cat—a real, live cat—and all sorts
of props: a fallout-shelter sign, record-album jackets, a copy of
Time. Dylan, one would gather, is an open-minded man. It's a
good show. One can study the photograph on the front of the
album for a long time: the hip baroque living-room setting; the
companion's pop frock (she looks like a Junior Miss Dragon
Lady); Dylan's shirt, with tab collar buttoned up tight, but not
garnished with a necktie. Somber-faced Dylan, supposedly surprised, has been interrupted, one takes it, from his meditations
on chaos, futility, and imperfection. Photographs on the back of
the album include Joan Baez, blowing on a harmonica; Peter
Yarrow (the Peter of Peter, Paul, and Mary), saluting two cops
by scratching his head; and Allen Ginsberg, the Beat poet, looking very fancy, like a racetrack dandy.

One cannot always tell an album by its jacket, but the main
photograph of BRINGING IT ALL BACK HOME suggests what to
expect inside, that is, weird but compelling poetic images strange-
ly set side by side in a manner generally known as surrealistic.
Like the artist Salvador Dali—who paints pictures involving limp
watches, fur-lined bathtubs, rhinoceros horns, and flaming gi-
raffes—Dylan maps the hidden country of his mind, the low roads
and byways of dreams and visions.

Here are samples of word-pictures from some of the album's
songs: *She Belongs to Me,* a lady who wears an Egyptian ring

RIGHT: *The portrait of a long-haired artist as folk-rock singer. Folk-rock swept
to international popularity near the end of 1965 with Dylan's songs* Subterranean Homesick Blues *and* Positively 4th Street. *As for long hair, Dylan has
jokingly said, "Obviously, if you get your hair on the outside of your head,
your brain will be a little more freer."*

that sparkles before she speaks; *On the Road Again,* frogs inside a pair of sox, a mother who hides inside an icebox, and a grandpa who has a cane that turns into a sword, a milkman who comes on wearing a derby hat. In *Bob Dylan's 115th Dream* he uses the surrealistic technique of mixing up time. Anachronisms include a ship, mastered by Captain A'rab (the Captain Ahab of MOBY DICK?), that makes a landfall in America where a cop throws captain and crew in jail for carrying harpoons and where protesters march along the Bowery carrying signs marked BAN THE BUMS, where a bowling ball rolls down a road, and where a foot pops out of a telephone.

Of course, not all of Dylan's visions are weirdly fantastic. Many make one think of the daydreams of childhood—the sort of things even you and I might have imagined, lying in the grass watching the clouds go by, or lying in the sand listening to the sounds of the seashore.

Dylan, it seems to me, has superb artistic control in BRINGING IT ALL BACK HOME. Sometimes he goes way, way out but never off the deep end. He keeps his feet on the ground by being humorous and by composing pleasing melodies. For an example of his lyrical talent, listen to the marvelously poetic images of *It's All Over Now, Baby Blue.* It's a song that says many things about the hopes and failures of our times, but equally important, it sounds beautiful throughout.

Poet, prophet, entertainer—Dylan is to my mind the most important figure in the world of popular songs. As of the mid-sixties he has set the best of the folk-song and rock 'n' roll musical styles to words that express what seems to be a spreading desire in America to attain personal freedom and to engage in some activity that a thinking person can believe in—something more than being a soldier, a shopkeeper, a corporation worker, or the like. However, Dylan, who has personal freedom (he is certainly worth more than a million dollars) and who unquestionably must believe in his art (the art of songwriting), does not tell us specifically how to be free or how to find an activity to believe in.

Unlike the Preacher of Ecclesiastes who, after concluding that "all is vanity," admonished, "Fear God, and keep his commandments; for this is the whole duty of man," Dylan does not admonish us to do anything. It will be interesting to see whether he ever does use his brilliant entertaining talent and poetic genius to tell us not just how bad things are but also what to do to make them better. I am not saying he should do that, because a good poet doesn't have to lead anybody anywhere.

While Dylan has turned to writing songs of personal poetry, other young men and women have continued a trend popular since the late fifties: the writing and singing of protest songs. They find a lot wrong with our world, and they believe many of us are uptight, shut off, abusive or abused. Their aim is to make us aware of hypocrisy, pretentiousness, stiffness, and foolishness. They are teachers, but instead of teaching in classrooms they generally attempt to enlighten us, guitar in hand, from the stages of coffeehouses. If a new protest song is particularly effective, it is likely to show up later in a record album; then we are able to take our lesson in the living room.

An example of a protest-song subject is suburbia: the land of the TV set, the big car for the family and the compact for shopping, but of hardly any Art or Literature; a land largely painted white, with only a black dot here and there: maids and gardeners.

Sometimes a lesson-in-song is so catchingly put together that it reaches people who would never think to look about them with a critical eye. That's the story of *Little Boxes,* a hit tune in 1964. Written by Malvina Reynolds, a pretty white-haired lady in her sixties, it takes a slap—part playful, part stinging—at housing developments, which the tune says are made of ticky tacky. The houses (little boxes) are all the same and the people in them are all the same too—all go to the university to become doctors, lawyers, and business executives; all play golf, drink their martinis dry; all send their pretty children to school, summer camp, to the university, and then into marriage and little boxes, all the same.

In writing the song, Malvina Reynolds knew firsthand what she was about. Living in Berkeley, she could see its university—in fact, she went there herself and received a Ph.D. in literature after writing a thesis about a medieval folktale—and she could see the housing developments which pockmark the San Francisco Bay area.

You might ask, "So, what's wrong with ticky tacky, with being a professional or a businessman, with drinking martinis dry, with playing golf, with having pretty children and sending them to summer camp, and so forth?" The answer is nothing and everything. It is good to live in comfort and to be and see pretty people —well dressed, with straight teeth—but it is bad when getting

Tom Paxton, a rare, short-haired folk singer, is famous for his protest song What Did You Learn in School Today? and the engrossing lullaby, Ramblin' Boy. Like Dylan and dozens of other folk singers, he has entertained audiences on both sides of the Atlantic.

things and keeping them means being like everybody else just about all the time. The trouble with ticky tacky is that you can't take a little bit, you have to swallow it all, whole and continually. Ticky-tacky town is where conformity reigns. Everybody is just about the same, in their work and in their play, but most important of all in their dreams. Those with unusual work (sculpturing, say) or unusual play (walking) don't get to suburbia, and those who are young and who aspire to the unusual leave suburbia as soon as they can, because they realize that something dies without the nourishment of variety.

A good album on which to hear *Little Boxes* is Pete Seeger's WE SHALL OVERCOME. Another good song in the album is one which takes a witty poke at how children are taught that everything is all right and that the world of grownups is just as it should be.

What Did You Learn in School Today? is addressed to a little boy. He learned, it turns out, what most of us learned and, to our sorrow, have since discovered to be half-truths—for example, that Washington never told a lie, that soldiers seldom die, that everybody's free, that war is not so bad.

It was written by Tom Paxton, who also wrote the lullaby *Ramblin' Boy* and hundreds of other songs. He, too, knows about the middle class, having been born to it in 1938. He spent most of his teens in Bristol, Oklahoma, a sleepy town, where he was raised by a widowed mother who had been left in comfortable circumstances. He studied drama at the University of Oklahoma, received a degree, and then served in the army. He began singing professionally in 1960 in the Gaslight, which issued his first album, now unavailable. Five years later, TOM PAXTON: RAMBLIN' BOY appeared. It's a good way to spend almost an hour's listening time.

NEWPORT BROADSIDE, which includes performances by Baez, Dylan, Phil Ochs, and Seeger, is another album with Paxton singing *Ramblin' Boy*. On the record he also sings *The Willing*

Conscript—certainly not a song that a recruiting sergeant would approve. A draftee sings to his instructor, "Now there are several lessons that I haven't mastered yet, / I haven't got the hang of how to use the bayonet, / If he doesn't die at once, sir, am I to stick him with it more? / Oh, I hope you will be patient / For I've never killed before."

Tom Paxton is one of an informal group of songwriters who perform in Greenwich Village and who publish songs in *Broadside,* the national monthly topical song magazine ($5 a year, 215 West 98th Street, Apt. 4-D, New York, N. Y. 10025). The Village writer-singers are numerous.

Among them I find Phil Ochs the most entertaining and enlightening. His songs bite and tickle and, sometimes, achieve beauty. He's a father, owns a car, talks sensible left-wing politics, prefers to drink orange juice and vodka, dresses as if he couldn't care less, and comes on with a straightforward, refreshing attitude about life in general and folk music in particular. Besides writing his own folk songs, he frequently writes letters and articles about his "purpose" and that of other composers and performers. For example, this paragraph written by him appeared in *Broadside #54:*

"With so many good writers around, the future of topical music clearly rests in many hands. And if you want to give credit where credit is due, I pay the greatest homage to Guy Carawan, who not only writes songs, but devotes his full time to the civil rights movement in the South, actively working in a real struggle, promoting workshops on how to use the music in the movement, and getting his banjo broken over his head on a picket line."

In the same article, Ochs also wrote, "My major concern is how honest and well-written I can make a song . . ."

Although many of Ochs' songs protest various injustices, he wrote in the September, 1965, issue of *Sing Out!:*

"I'm not getting on stage to mouth the correct political images whether they're based on logic or not. I'm not out there to be a

"Mississippi" Phil Ochs, so called because of his caustic song about that state, is America's foremost protester. The best of his anti-Establishment songs were performed at a Carnegie Hall debut before an enthusiastic full house in January, 1966. He also contributes satirical essays to The Realist *and* Cavalier.

spokesman for the Left, for SNCC [the Student Nonviolent Co-ordinating Committee], for my generation, or for anybody but myself."

Ochs also is a big Dylan booster and a defender of Dylan's switch from writing protest songs to personal ones. In a letter to the *Village Voice,* August 12, 1965, Ochs wrote:

"I can't emphasize strongly enough that there must be no shackles put on any writer to force him to cover certain subject material or use certain styles. Dylan is being violently criticized for using amplified rock 'n' roll as his medium on the Newport folk stage. Just wait and see if we invite you again next year Bobby Teenybopper. I can just imagine some of the cops at Newport who happened to be folk purists reaching for their holsters muttering, 'That's not folk music.' "

As this excerpt makes obvious, Ochs is by no means a folk-song purist; although he himself plays an unamplified guitar, he is an enthusiast of rock 'n' roll and of country-and-western. He thinks it more important that songs be entertaining than that they have a social message.

Songs of his which are both entertaining and have a social message that I especially like include:

Talking Cuban Crisis—"Here comes the President / But first this word from Pepsodent: / Have whiter teeth, have cleaner breath / when you are facing nuclear death . . . / Now, most Americans stood behind the President and his military minds / But me, I stood behind a bar, dreaming of a spaceship getaway car . . ."

Talking Vietnam—in which the deposed and assassinated President Diem says, "The family that slays together stays together."

There but for Fortune—"Show me the whiskey that stains on / the floor. / Show me the drunkard as he stumbles / out the door, / And I'll show you a young man with many / reasons why, / And there but for fortune may go you / or I."

Two albums recorded by Phil Ochs are ALL THE NEWS THAT'S FIT TO SING and I AIN'T MARCHING ANYMORE.

Buffy Sainte-Marie is quite quotable—for example, "My music comes from the soles of my feet" and "I love to sing, love the way it feels, the sensual feeling of song in my throat." Her songs and the way she sings them substantiate these statements. Hers is an unusual sound, generally not beautiful, often haunting, and always full of the passion that is absent in the singing of Joan Baez. Buffy Sainte-Marie songs create an intimate mood. They're womanly. You get the feeling she means it. On her first album, IT'S MY WAY, the song *Co'dine,* a warning against addiction, is hypnotically frightening and, therefore, fascinating. On the same album, *Now That the Buffalo's Gone* is a touching statement about the continual treachery worked against the red man. She dedicates the song to the late Peter LaFarge. He, like Buffy, was of Indian descent. And he, too, was a folk-song writer (for example, *Ira Hayes,* a song made popular by Johnny Cash). In *Sing Out!* of March, 1965—eight months before his death at the age of thirty-four—he had this to say about her:

"Buffy, I can say with truth, is a very fine authority on the American Indian . . . It is very difficult to grow up ashamed and shy among your schoolmates because you're strange and different and alien, then to find pride and strength from the very disaster of your people and carry it with you as first concern in an overcrowded heart."

Another descendant of the American Indians writing and singing folk songs is Patrick Sky. He could well be the hillbilly humorist in the city. Here's a segment of a letter he wrote to Sis Cunningham, the elderly lady who edits *Broadside:*

Buffy Sainte-Marie, the Cree Indian who says, "When I'm old and have no figure and no long hair and an ancient face, then I will still be singing," is the composer of haunting and passionate songs including Co'dine, *which is about the pitfalls of addiction, and* Universal Soldier, *an indictment of all fighting men. Her artistry has been given the seal of approval in the form of fan-type picture stories which appeared in* Look *and* Life *magazines.*

The late Peter LaFarge made a haunting contribution to the American heritage. A onetime boxer and rodeo rider, he was an intense and sincere writer of both songs and articles protesting the oppressions suffered by Indians and exposing the hypocrisies of contemporary society.

"Dear Sis—You asked me to write an article. I don't know much about writing—it's all I can do to read. I was born in a house in the glorious city of Live Oak Gardens, Georgia. My mother is of Creek lineage and my father was Cherokee and Irish. I guess that makes me part white. Just what percentage of blood I have is a mystery to me. I would guess 93/42nds.

"I was raised in the country by a wood stove and no electricity to speak of. I went to school five miles away, to which I had to walk five miles every morning. My whole family plays an instrument of some sort. Mom plays guitar, I played a banjo—four strings—and Dad played guitar also. I used to sing at dances when I was six years old, for money—two dollars, to be exact. I also sang for the Lord every Sunday at the little old First Christian Church; this I did for free—after all, one can't take nothing from the Lord.

"The years went by and we moved all over the South, living in such detested places as Meridian, Mississippi; Monroe, Louisiana; Houston, Texas; and God knows how many other places. Finally I got old and went into the Army for a two year stretch. After I got out, I went to college for three months. I moved back to Georgia and met Ernie Marrs. I had been playing all along, but it was Ernie who got me on the road to try and make a go of it. I played pizza palaces, barn dances, fraternities (yech!), and last but not least, coffeehouses.

"All my life I have been trying to learn to be a good musician and get away from my country accent and background. When I came North, everyone was trying to get a country accent and learn to play country music. Boy! did that twist my head. I still haven't adjusted to it."

For a laughing song, listen to Patrick Sky's *Give to the Cause* (". . . give us a share / Give to the cause,—help make us a millionaire") a spoof of the ever-present charity-fund drives. It is in BROADSIDE SINGERS VOL. 3, an album which includes, among fourteen original compositions, *Welcome, Welcome Emigrante* by Buffy Sainte-Marie and *Rattlesnake*, a powerful and catchy song by Peter LaFarge.

Moreover, the album is important because it includes Len Chandler. He sings his song *Father's Grave*. It's beautiful, as is much of what Chandler writes and sings. It's ironic, but it wasn't until late in 1965 that a company decided to record him on an album all his own. It sometimes happens that recording companies just can't accept talent even when it is shoved at them. Sooner or later, in Chandler's case, it had to happen, though. He was just too good to be ignored forever. He has a polished style, which, with the exception of Buffy Sainte-Marie and a few others,

is not *the* thing in folk singing. He's also sophisticated—actually writes love songs which are sensual—which is also not the thing; not yet, anyhow.

But Chandler, who is in his late twenties, who went to the University of Akron, who played with the Akron Symphony, who received a master's degree in music from Columbia University,

The piper in this striking
tableau reminiscent of the
American Revolution but
photographed during the civil
rights march on Montgomery,
Alabama, in 1965 is Len
Chandler — a singer and
writer of timely and engaging
songs.

could achieve mass popularity. Who knows if he'll debut in Carnegie Hall or have a hit on the jukeboxes? Nobody, for sure.
When his album is released by Columbia Records his star may
rise; meanwhile, he can be heard live. If you get the opportunity,
listen.

Getting out of the living room and into the coffeehouse or concert hall is always a good idea. Hearing a professional on records is fine, but hearing one live is sometimes better. Then, too, there is an added inducement: listening and singing along with other *folks.* You can't beat it.

The songs created by coffeehouse folk musicians, the social-protest attitudes of performers and audiences, and the casual appearance of both have been severely taken to task by several critics. These criticisms deserve consideration.

The November, 1964, issue of *HiFi/Stereo Review* carried an article titled "The Folk-Music Bomb: In which our critic delivers himself of some intemperate opinions on the subject of contemporary folk music and folk music musicians." The blurb makes it obvious that the editor was made uneasy by writer Gene Lees' sweeping attack.

Lees charges that "folkies"—a term he says jazz musicians use to describe synthetic folk singers—write unpoetic lyrics on subjects they know nothing about. He seems to think that poetry can be nothing else but the King's English, rhymed to a strict meter. He also implies great delight with the tradition of musical-comedy lyrics, but would deny the right of current folk-song writers to make use of a long American tradition of protest against joblessness, union busting, and so forth.

Dig him being facetious:

"Trains are always good in folk songs. Also hunger, lonesomeness, homelessness, the land (even if all you've ever seen of it is Central Park), the open sky, long roads, being out of work, girl friends who died, and what a drag the Establishment is. Jails are very good, too—really *in* this year. The fact that you're fresh out of Brooklyn College and have never seen the outside of a jail, much less the inside, shouldn't deter you. And, of course, it is requisite that you protest—against unfairness, injustice, and that kind of stuff."

A little more protest *against that kind of stuff,* especially if compellingly done, might go a long way toward straightening out our mix-ups. And since when has a composer had to have direct experience about a subject in order to write a song about it? Consider the Tin Pan Alley lyricist sitting in Manhattan dreaming up happy lines about catchy situations involving Gary, Indiana, and River City, Idaho; consider how, at times, he comes right down on the stereotype of the good-old, good-time days with the librarian waiting for the simple, true man as the smell of apple pie wafts about the old clapboard house—the one surrounded by the white picket fence. Really, who cares whether the composer has never been west of East Orange?

Nevertheless, for what it is worth, Lees' point has been taken. More and more folk-song writers concentrate on what comes out of their own lives. Dylan projects in his personal hang-ups the tensions and disappointments of lots of kids; and others draw on their personal experiences, whether from childhood, or college days, whether in suburbia or the cities. Meanwhile, Phil Ochs and other Broadsiders focus on immediate political and social problems that stir their imaginations.

Lees also charges that this sort of protest song is no good because it is both shallow and short lived. *Talking Vietnam* could not do the work of a full-length book exposé of that mess, but Ochs' satirical jabs sure get to the point quickly. To cite another example, *Blowin' in the Wind* in three minutes is a great deal more effective as a call to freedom and dignity than any number of hour-long Fourth of July speeches or commencement addresses.

Lees says, "What is not seen by the folkies is that when art is chained to temporary social problems, it can only be temporary art—its value persists only as long as the problem it protests." Yes. So? "Sufficient unto the day is the evil thereof." If a handful of the thousands of songs being written now are sung a hundred years from now, so much the better for the people listening then.

A folk-song writer would be a fool to worry about whether his art will last. The problem is communication now. It's really unimportant to us if Bob Dylan turns out not to have the lasting appeal of Johannes Brahms, an earlier folk-song adapter.

Another of Lees' complaints is that folk songs are one-sided—on the side of the underdog and never on the side of the rich and the powerful. He's right. The reason for this bias was made clear by the Reverend Howard Moody, pastor of Greenwich Village's Judson Memorial Church, when he explained why he and his congregation supported folk singers in Washington Square. (The Washington Square battle is described in Chap. 8.) In a sermon on May 7, 1961, the Reverend Moody said:

"If you claim that our concerns seem a little one-sided I can only quote one of the preachers of our tradition who insists that partiality for the needy is at the heart of the Biblical notion of justice: 'His delight will be in the fear of the Lord / He will not judge by that which his eyes see / Nor decide by that which his ears hear / But with JUSTICE will he judge the needy / And with FAIRNESS decide for the poor of the land.' "

Finally, Lees claims that some folk singers are trying to get into the pop music field and are failing because "The majority have bad time, a poor sense of phrasing, bad vocal sound, uncontrolled and thin vibrato, no sustaining power, no ear for harmony—a veritable catalog of musical defects that will assure them early and total eclipse in the pops field."

Now, Lees is no more concerned than I am that *some* folk singers can't make it as pop singers. Many are called but few are chosen. In any case, what Lees implies is that coffeehouse singers are to be condemned because they don't have the spit and polish

LEFT: *Like other folk-song writers of the "protest" type, Phil Ochs takes every opportunity to musically proclaim the personal hang-ups, the tensions and disappointments of a lot of kids, high-school and college age. Listeners are never hard to find.*

of supper-club singers. Once again, so? What he is trying to do is to say that apples are better than pears. It's easy to reverse the process and say that if some folk singers can't make it as pop singers, some pop singers can't make it as folk singers.

Folk songs at their best are sincere attempts to express emotion about deeply felt matters, some of them public, some personal. It's hard to be sincere and honest; many failures occur. It's easy to make fun of the failures. Glib writers, the Sunday-supplement kind, can't resist the temptation. Here, for example, are the words of the late Robert C. Ruark, novelist and columnist:

". . . somehow the simple folkers have managed to legislate an aura of art around what can charitably be called nothing better than a public nuisance. And when the urge to do good becomes insupportable, they dust off the folk dancers and ship 'em to the downtrodden to convince the poor in spirit that we are a nation of rubes and hilltop yodelers.

"We are not a nation of Hirams, completely—or at least I'm not, and I think I constitute a majority. Drive the folk singers underground, is what I say, for underground is where they belong."

Mr. Ruark attained middle age and shut himself off. A common enough condition among the majority, is it not?

Moreover, it doesn't happen often that a song is created that can really touch us deeply. Nor can every singer be exceptional. Singing is for all who want to try and for all who get pleasure from it. Any number can play. Millions do, and a portion of those make up their own songs, which is fine. Of those who write songs and sing them, hopefully for pay, some struggle awhile to keep alive ("passing the basket," it's called) and then take up other pursuits; some have a short burst of popularity only to fade into oblivion; a few gather a following, make a living, and continue to hope for the big strike; fewer still achieve fame, and of those, fewer than half a dozen not only have entertained us but have helped change our way of looking at life.

🕉 3 Hard Traveling

Tall, lanky, strong-featured, twinkling-faced Pete Seeger, folk singer uniformed in a bulky sweater, picked a banjo and sang of the polluted Hudson River.

Inaugurating *Broadside*'s first topical-song workshop (Sunday, November 1, 1964), his song filled the Village Gate, a chamber (called in a different milieu a rathskeller) off the corner of Bleecker Street and a few steps in on Thompson Street, reached by going down a narrow flight of stairs and past a two-dollar ticket taker.

He sang to an audience predominantly young—thirteen, fourteen . . . twenty-four, twenty-five or so—that looked well fed and, presumably, well schooled; relaxed, not stiff. The girls wore straight skirts or tight slacks, sweaters, blouses, a dress now and then; most had long straight hair (no bouffants). The boys were in khaki and denim, corduroy. There were even city suits—at least two (the gentleman—middle-aged—from the press and the young executive, possibly a recording company representative). Warm not cool. Here and there a bottle of beer, occasionally a glass of scotch. Laughter for the funny metaphors; attentive quiet for the biting message; clapping and tapping for the beat. Almost every face white, except on the stage.

On the stage: Julius Lester, bespectacled, thin, intense, a guitar teacher and a writer of songs which he hopes will help keep alive the Negro tradition of folk music. Bernice Reagon, a little lady with a big beautiful voice, a former member of the Student Non-violent Coordinating Committee's Freedom Singers, and the wife of Cordell Reagon, a current Freedom Singer; Eric Anderson, a *Broadside* contributor and writer of *Plains of Nebrasky-O*. Len Chandler, Phil Ochs, Tom Paxton, Buffy Sainte-Marie, Patrick Sky. All in all, a fairly good cross section of modern folk singers.

Pete Seeger sings another song. Everybody joins in, the audience in front, waiting performers behind him. It's Pete Seeger in a situation where he cannot be excelled: leading others in song.

Pete Seeger has been singing folk songs for pay—when he could get it or when he wasn't contributing to a charity or a cause—for three decades. At how many concerts and hootenannies and over how many radio broadcasts nobody knows. Safe enough to say, though, that he has sung more folk music to more people all over the world than any other performer. And he's done it well.

RIGHT: *Pete Seeger, at forty-six, has been singing for thirty years to always enthusiastic and ever-growing numbers of fans. His concert appearances, international tours, and records have made him famous. Although long ostracized by television, in the winter 1965–66 season he appeared regularly on his own program, "Rainbow Quest," over New York's Channel 47. The name of the program is the title of one of his own songs. Other popular songs he wrote include* Turn, Turn, Turn *and* Where Have All the Flowers Gone?

Nobody seems to know how many LP solo albums he's made (somewhere between forty and fifty is Seeger's guess), let alone the total number of records he's appeared on with other performers.

No matter. For an album that gives an idea how he can get people to sing, listen to WITH VOICES TOGETHER WE SING. It, and especially the South African song *Wimoweh,* should be heard by every schoolteacher in the whole wide world. I only wish the principal at old Public School #13 in Valley Stream, Long Island, could have heard it. Maybe then he would have put away his long wooden pointer—which he waved out of time, anyway. Maybe he would have taken up the banjo. It tickles me to imagine that stiff old gentleman picking away, foot tapping, and voice ripping out with a Seeger-style yodel. I'll tell you one thing: we would have enjoyed the weekly assembly.

However, make no mistake, Pete Seeger is not universally appreciated as a performer. He even criticizes himself for being "uneven." In *Sing Out!* (March, 1965), he wrote a critique of his own artistry which says in part:

". . . Taken all together [the recorded works] form one of the most horrendously uneven bodies of music that any performer could boast of . . .

". . . Scattered throughout the discs, you will occasionally hear some passable ballad singing.

". . . If you like the blues, don't even bother listening . . . [This holds true for all white folks who try to sing the blues. None, but none, can compare with a good Negro blues singer.]

". . . In between two pretty good songs [on any of his albums] is sandwiched a sentimental little piece of nothing."

Although he exaggerates, there's much to what he says concerning the last point (judging from the Seeger albums I've heard). What's more, he's often just not very exciting. For example, on PETE SEEGER AND SONNY TERRY the only kick comes from Sonny's singing and harmonica playing.

With such self-criticism, there is little danger that Pete Seeger will permit himself to be turned into a totem. That's good, for too many artists, politicians, and business magnates have accepted too much praise and have done too little soul-searching.

Still, there's no reason to go overboard. What *Time* magazine said about Seeger, for example, is not true, "His voice sounds as if a cornstalk were stuck in his throat." Seeger has an adequate, pleasing voice which he uses well.

More to the point, Seeger is an entertaining pitchman for the causes of liberty, equality, and fraternity. He can praise and condemn in a way that touches the liberal mind. Nice people like him, and nice people—college age especially—are even capable of feeling and sounding militant during the several hours he performs before them.

His reputation as a champion of liberty is based on a quarter century of defending his own civil liberties and those of others. To understand him it is necessary to review how he and some politicians, super patriots, and frightened TV executives clashed.

Pete Seeger was born in 1919 in New York City. (His father is a musicologist, conductor, author, and educator and his mother, a violinist and teacher.) He went to Harvard for two years and then rambled around the country for several more learning songs and singing them. Both before and after serving in the army during World War II (he sang for soldiers in the United States and the South Pacific), he performed with other folk singers at hootenannies—at that time affairs held to raise funds for political purposes or to organize laborers into unions. During the fifties he ran into all kinds of trouble because of these performances and others which were sometimes for causes favored by the Communist party. Those who supported these causes were sometimes

In coffeehouses the world over a generation of performers and their audiences relate to folk singing in a style fashioned by Pete Seeger.

called fellow travelers, sometimes Commies, and sometimes Reds. They were baited, chased, questioned, told to squeal or pay the consequences, which ranged from loss of a job (even if it was only a janitor's) to imprisonment. The baiting was carried out in some corporations, some universities, some school districts. It was carried out by city, state, and the Federal Government (to protect the national security, said the investigators, during the Cold War with the Russians), by the American Legion, and by legislators, such as Senator Joseph McCarthy and members of the House Committee on Un-American Activities.

People in high and low places were oppressed. An old cleaning woman lost her job at an air-force base. Professor Owen Lattimore, at one time America's foremost authority on the Far East, was questioned, harassed, and finally driven from the country. J. Robert Oppenheimer, a physicist who led scientists in developing the atomic bomb, was denied security clearance and disgraced. (Later, the injustice was indirectly acknowledged when President Johnson "on the part of the American people" presented Oppenheimer with the $50,000 Enrico Fermi Award.) In the fifties, even school officials were nervous, and in some high schools, before being permitted to graduate, students were required to sign loyalty oaths proclaiming that the signer had never been a member of an organization advocating the overthrow of the United States Government.

A few men and women stood up to the Red-hunters. But many more either lacked courage or didn't much believe in the civil liberties proclaimed by the Constitution.

Senator Joseph McCarthy—an irresponsible, unprincipled, political cad—went berserk. Meanwhile, much of the nation cowered, or, at least, kept frighteningly quiet—that is, until he held hearings about suspected (by him) subversion in the United States Army. The hearings were televised, and they were watched as if they were the World Series. The Secretary of the Army and various brass called to testify showed something less than backbones of steel—squashed banana would be more descriptive. One exception was a country-style lawyer from Massachusetts, Robert Welch. He accomplished what the biggest general of them all, Dwight David Eisenhower, didn't even try to do—even though he was President of the United States. Welch threw a block at wild-running Joe. A sigh of relief, if not a cheer, seemed to go up from the nation.

Later, the Senate told Senator McCarthy that he had been behaving badly. He slowed down, shut up, and shortly after died.

Gradually, all over the nation, Red-baiting declined—especially when relations with the Russians improved in the sixties; it declined, but it didn't end: certainly not for Pete Seeger. His road, for a while, remained a hard one.

Citing the First Amendment to the Constitution, he refused to testify before the Committee on Un-American Activities about his political beliefs and associations dating back to the forties. He was convicted for contempt of Congress in 1961. He appealed, and, while the outcome of the appeal was uncertain, a number of folk singers stood up for his right of free speech. Joan Baez, for example, at her every performance, dedicated a song to him.

The following year, Pete Seeger's conviction was reversed.

But his troubles continued.

In April, 1963, the ABC-TV network launched a program called, of all things, "Hootenanny," and, even more remarkable, it blacklisted Pete Seeger.

"Hootenanny," never much of a television show, folded after a year. It wasn't much as far as folk music goes either. First Joan Baez and then other performers refused to participate. She said, "No Seeger, no Baez." Bob Dylan said, "No Seeger, no Dylan." The same message came from a number of other singers.

Meanwhile, Seeger took his family—wife, three children, and father-in-law—on a singing tour of Africa, Asia, Australia, and Europe. The tour, made without the sponsorship of any government agency, was a great success.

He and his entourage returned to the small town of Beacon, New York—about an hour's travel time from Manhattan—the base from which he continues to help build a healthy musical life for people everywhere, both through his own playing and songwriting and by encouraging talented young singers and songwriters. ("Most of us owe our careers to Pete," Joan Baez has said.)

His own performances are generally able, often excellent, never arty, and occasionally he even manages to swing. (Hear *Oh, Freedom* on WE SHALL OVERCOME.) Several songs of his authorship have been commercially successful. For example, *Where Have All the Flowers Gone?* was a hit in this country and abroad —Marlene Dietrich's version sold more than three hundred thousand records in Germany. His books, such as HOW TO PLAY THE FIVE-STRING BANJO, have also done well.

Seeger comes from a three-hundred-year-old New England line of religious dissenters, of Revolutionary War soldiers, of Civil War abolitionists. This heritage is apparent close up. One can feel righteousness combined with flinty strength and another quality rare in our society: saintliness as composed of selflessness, self-confidence, dedication, courage, and charisma.

He sings, he gets others to sing; possibly through his songs he influences people, certainly he entertains them.

A man whom, as far as I know, no one has ever likened to a saint, but who nevertheless has the status of a hero and the influence of a prophet is Woody Guthrie.

He was born Woodrow Wilson Guthrie on July 14, 1912, in Okemah, Oklahoma, which according to Woody "was one of the singingest, square dancingest, drinkingest, yellingest, preachingest, waltzingest, talkingest, laughingest, cryingest, shootingest, fist fightingest, bleedingest, gamblingest, gun, club and razor carryingest of our ranch towns, because it blossomed out into one of our first oil boom towns." His father played the guitar, got into lots of fist fights, speculated in real estate, went broke, and moved himself and members of his family—not always together—to various parts of the Southwest. Woody's mother, in his words, "was an ear musician . . . Songs meant a lot to her and she collected hundreds of them in her head, and she chorded on the piano and sung tales and stories that taught me the history of our section of the country, its weather, cyclones, pretty women, love affairs, disasters and its outlaws." She kept house (two of which were destroyed by fire and another by a cyclone), had a nervous breakdown, and eventually died in an insane asylum. Meanwhile, Woody and his brother and sisters grew up, except the one sister who died of burns she received in the explosion of an oil stove.

The family broke up. Woody went out on his own. In his early teens, he learned the guitar from an uncle in Texas. He sang at carnivals, country dances, rodeos, and in saloons and later over radio stations in California and Mexico. Meanwhile, he had gotten married—the first of three times. The Depression was on. Woody saw poverty in the cities and in the migratory camps. Traveling by rail—mostly in boxcars, but sometimes on top of them—he rambled east and west. In New York City he wrote a column for the *Daily Worker*.

Pete Seeger has this to say about that period and his long association with Guthrie:

"I first met Woody Guthrie in the fall of 1939. It was at a folk song evening in New York City, held on the stage of a Broadway theater, right after the regular theater audience had gone. It was a midnight benefit to try to raise money for some of the California migratory workers . . . there was Woody, a little short fellow with a Western hat and boots, in blue jeans and needing a shave, spinning out stories and singing songs that he had made up himself. . . . I think I learned so many different things from Woody that I can hardly count them. His ability to identify with the ordinary man and woman, speak their own language without using the fancy words, and never be afraid—no matter where you were; just diving into some situation, trying it out. He and I used to go around singing together. CIO Union, all kinds of places. Churches, saloons, meetings, parties . . . I remember the night he wrote the song *Tom Joad*. He said, 'Pete do you know where I can get a typewriter?' I said, 'I'm staying with someone who has one.' 'Well, I got to write a ballad,' he said. 'I don't usually write ballads to order, but Victor wants me to do a whole album of Dust Bowl songs, and they say they want one about Tom Joad, the character in the movie *The Grapes of Wrath.*' I asked him if he had read the book, and he said, 'No, but I went and saw the movie. Good movie.' So he went along to the place I was staying—six flights walking up—and it was really a long walk-up on East 45th Street. The friend I was staying with said, 'Sure, you can use my typewriter.' Woody had a half-gallon jug of wine with him, and sat down and started typing away. Stand up every few seconds and test out a verse on his guitar and sit down and type some more. About one o'clock I and my friend, we got so sleepy we couldn't

Woody Guthrie, long too sick to sing or write, is the friend of Pete Seeger and the mentor of Bob Dylan and Jack Elliott. He has influenced almost every other professional folk performer. John Steinbeck says that he embodies the "American spirit."

stay awake and we were lost. In the morning, we woke up and
there was Woody curled up on the floor under the table; the half-
gallon of wine was almost empty and the completed ballad was
sitting near the typewriter. And it is still one of his masterpieces.
. . . Woody was like Popeye: I am what I am, what I am, and I
ain't gonna change. He was going to cuss, he was going to shock
people, but he was going to stay the way he was. He wasn't going
to let New York make him sick and sleek and contented. He was
going to stay a rebel until the end. Not that he was always angry
—Lord, no, he was one of the happiest people. He was always
ready with a joke, but if he felt mad about something, he would
come out and say it. He wasn't polite at all. And that kind of
honesty—boy, you have to take off your hat to. It cost him a lot
of jobs. He had a job on the Model Tobacco program for $200 a
week in 1940 (early 1940) and he could have been very well off
for many a year to come, but they wanted him to fit into their
groove of popular singer and he didn't see it that way, so he lasted
about a month or two with them and then he quit it. . . . I remember once Woody went to a party in Pennsylvania—cocktail party
—people weren't really interested in listening to anything, and he
sang one song and the chatter kept on going. He sang another
song and they kept on chattering, so, in the middle of his third
song he stopped, slung the guitar on his back, walked over to the
table where the whiskey was, picked up two full quarts of whiskey, one in each hand, and walked out the door. The hostess, I
understand, never got over it. She said, 'That man!' She just
assumed that he'd be like any cocktail pianist, I suppose, and just
make a pleasant rattle in the background. . . . I think that, of
Woody's thousands of songs and verses, quite a large number are
going to outlive this century, and that is a rare thing for a songwriter. . . . I think that maybe several dozen of Woody's songs are
going to be sung by my grandchildren and their grandchildren."

I don't know which of Woody's songs will be sung by Pete

Seeger's grandchildren's grandchildren, but those that are most popular now are *Hard Travelin'; Pastures of Plenty; So Long, It's Been Good to Know You; This Land Is Your Land*. It is inconceivable that there is a professional folk singer who at one time or another has not sung one of these or other of Woody's songs. But besides singing his songs, other folk singers have been influenced by the *way* he sings and writes.

Bob Dylan's first album, for example, throbs with the sounds of Woody—especially the harmonica sound. And in many of the talking blues and album jacket notes that Dylan has written, it is easy to detect a direct link to such passages as:

"Some people liked me, hated me, walked with me, walked over me, jeered me, cheered me, rooted me and hooted me, and before long I was invited in and booted out of every public place of entertainment in that country. But I decided that the songs was a music and a language of all tongues.

"I never did make up many songs about the cow trails or the moon skipping through the sky, but at first it was funny songs of what all's wrong, and how it turned out good or bad. Then I got a little braver and made up songs telling what I thought was wrong and how to make it right, songs that said what everybody in that country was thinking."

This quotation is from Woody's autobiographical BOUND FOR GLORY, first published in 1943 and now available in a paperback Dolphin Book. A chapter titled "Cain't No Gang Whip Us Now" is a superb piece of writing about childhood—about building a fort, a treetop observation tower, and country-kid gang fights. The book is pretty good when it comes to sex, too. Nothing shocking. Just artful and, to me anyway, truthful. A fine book.

In 1965 Macmillan published BORN TO WIN: *a collection of stories, drawings, letters, poems, and snatches by America's greatest prophet-singer, fascist-killer, folk-poet, talker, hummer, whistler, dancer, rambler, fighter, and all-time balladeer hero*. It is edited by Robert Shelton, under assignment by the Guthrie Trust Fund. (The Fund was established in 1956, a year after Woody became critically ill with Huntington's chorea, a nervous disease of which his mother died. Royalties are collected on his songs and writings to help provide for his children.) According to trustees of the Fund, BORN TO WIN is but a small part of Woody's unpublished material; they plan to have additional books put together in the next few years.

In 1966 Woody is still a patient at Brooklyn State Hospital. Visits are not encouraged, although his immediate family and close friends see him regularly.

Millard Lampell, an editor of Woody's songs and other writings, was a member, with Pete Seeger and Woody, of the Almanac Singers, a group which sang before factory and farm laborers in the early forties. He has edited another work titled BOUND FOR GLORY, this one a Folkways album of thirteen Guthrie songs. Two other albums worth hearing are DUST BOWL BALLADS and the LIBRARY OF CONGRESS RECORDINGS. In discussing the entire body of Woody's songs, Lampell praises them as effectively as I suppose anybody can. He says that they are:

". . . songs with love in them, songs with loneliness and sorrow in them, songs with a fierce and stubborn will to survive. Some of them were played on every radio station and jukebox in the country. And some of them were hummed and whistled and passed along until they became part of the weave of the life of this land. And people would swear to you that they were old folk songs, drifted up through the hickory smoke of history."

Another articulate appreciator is Nobel Prize winner John Steinbeck, who has written of Woody:

"He sings the songs of a people, and I suspect that he is, in a way, that people. Harsh voiced and nasal, his guitar banging like a tire iron on a rusty rim, there is nothing sweet about Woody, and there is nothing sweet about the songs he sings. But there is

Cisco Houston, who took his first name from a Sierra Nevada town not far from the Donner Pass and who traveled the nation by means of the sunburned thumb and the side-door Pullman, was a several-time-torpedoed sailor during World War II and a singer of folk songs for more than two decades. He died in 1961.

something more important for those who will listen. There is the will of a people to endure and fight against oppression. I think we call this the American spirit."

For a man so long out of the performing spotlight, Woody casts a long shadow. In 1962 THE OTHER AMERICA, Michael Harrington's book about poverty, appeared. Chapter Three, titled "Pastures of Plenty" and devoted to the sufferings of migratory workers, includes the words of Woody's song of the same title. This is just one of countless examples of how Woody has become a prophet recognized both in his own country and in his own time.

A special friend of Woody, a traveling companion and fellow singer, was Cisco (Gilbert Vañdiñe) Houston, who was born in Wilmington, Delaware, on August 18, 1918, and who died of cancer April 28, 1961, in San Bernardino, California. During the Depression, Cisco, like Woody, had many odd jobs, including pickle-factory worker, movie bit-part player, seaman, theater actor, and singer. Woody tells of their first meeting:

"I run into a guitar-playing partner standing on a bad corner, and he called his self the Cisco Kid. He was a long-legged guy that walked like he was on a rolling ship, a good singer and yodeler, and had sailed the seas a lot of times, busted labels [drank booze] in a lot of ports, and he had really been around in his twenty-six years. He banged on the guitar pretty good, and like me, come rain or shine, or cold or heat, he always walked along with his guitar slung over his shoulder from a leather strap."

It was a meeting that resulted in a long-term friendship, and one that deeply affected Cisco's singing. A Hollywood-handsome man with a dashing mustache, Cisco had a rich baritone voice, and he sang hundreds of songs all over the United States and a good part of the rest of the world. He made many records, the best of those I've heard being, appropriately, CISCO HOUSTON SINGS THE SONGS OF WOODY GUTHRIE.

Others who sang during Woody's performing years, who sang his songs and felt his presence, include John Greenway and Jack Elliott.

Greenway is a musical scholar who holds a Phi Beta Kappa key and a Ph.D. received after writing a dissertation titled "American Folksongs of Social and Economic Protest." On THE GREAT

AMERICAN BUM, he sings, in a pleasing, unpretentious voice, nineteen hobo and migratory workers' songs. I know of no better folk-song album. Four of the songs are Woody's: *Ramblin'*, *Bonneville Dam, Hard Travelin'*, and *The Hobo's Lullaby*. (In Greenway's introduction to the album he explains that "a hobo is a migratory worker, a tramp is a migratory non-worker, and a bum is a stationary non-worker.")

Jack Elliott, with his "Marlboro Country" face, is a colorful, funny, smarter-than-you'd-first-think man who wears relaxed-looking, good-fitting clothes, cowboy boots, and a black Stetson hat. He was born in Brooklyn in 1931, but he doesn't talk much about Brooklyn, at least not publicly, for, like Dylan, Jack publicly cut the ties with his family. Jack assumed as many of Woody's

Jack Elliott, an engaging young man often seen wearing cowboy hat and boots and steel-rimmed glasses, possesses an exceptionally entertaining talent. He is not as well known or as financially successful as he might be. Singing professionally only for his keep and that of his family, he otherwise follows his fancy—be it sailing schooners, riding broncs, or talking away the night.

characteristics as possible, especially his singing and speaking styles and his attitudes about living. Jack met Woody in 1951 in New York City. For as long as he could he stayed close to the great man, listening and learning, until at one point Woody said, "Jack sounds more like me than I do." (Years after Woody went to the hospital, Bob Dylan—fresh from the Midwest—visited and absorbed as much as he could of the master's style. Jack, who had been through it all, remembers how he smiled to himself at what the new fellow was up to.)

Jack went off to England and the Continent, where to enthusiastic audiences he introduced Woody's songs, including *1913 Massacre, Ludlow,* and *Pretty Boy Floyd.*

To hear what Robert Shelton has called "the droning, ambling, low-pressured tobacco-chewing casualness of a plainsman crooning to his horse—or his girl," listen to the man at his best on an album titled simply JACK ELLIOTT. As for his live performances, Jack is a pure entertainer in a field heavy with purpose and peppered with political pretense. He doesn't sing protest songs, at least not ones about current events. This is one of the differences between Jack Elliott and Pete Seeger. What they have in common is exceptional talent as folk singers. Pete's place is recognized widely; although it's risky to speculate, I believe Jack's will be.

Besides Woody, there are two other legendary folk singers: Joe Hill and Leadbelly.

On November 18, 1915 this will was written:

"My will is easy to decide,/ For there is nothing to divide./ My kin don't need to fuss and moan—/'Moss does not cling to a rolling stone.'/ My body?—Oh!—If I could choose,/ I would to ashes it reduce,/ And let the merry breezes blow/ My dust to where some flowers grow./ Perhaps some fading flower then/ Would come to life and bloom again./ This is my last and final will,/ Good luck to all of you,/ Joe Hill."

The next day, before a five-man firing squad in Utah State Penitentiary shot him dead, Joe Hill sent two telegrams to Big Bill Haywood, head of the Wobblies, officially known as the Industrial Workers of the World—the I.W.W. "Good-bye, Bill. I die like a true-blue rebel. Don't waste any time in mourning. Organize." And, "It is only a hundred miles from here to Wyoming. Could you arrange to have my body hauled to the state line to be buried? I don't want to be found dead in Utah."

The execution has been immortalized in a song titled simply *Joe Hill* by Earl Robinson and Alfred Hayes. (Hear the album SONGS OF JOE HILL BY JOE GLAZER.) Its first verse goes: "I dreamed I saw Joe Hill last night/ Alive as you and me,/ Says I, 'But, Joe, you're ten years dead.'/ 'I never died,' says he./ 'I never died,' says he."

The Robinson and Hayes song has it that "the copper bosses killed you Joe . . ."

Joe Hill got the I.W.W. to sing. His songs were printed on cards and in a little red songbook. They were sung in hobo jungles, jails, picket lines, and by sailors on American ships all over the world. As a Wobbly, Joe Hill had one aim: the One Big Union and the Cooperative Commonwealth which would be free of class and nationality distinctions. The State of Utah, in fact, killed Joe Hill because he allegedly murdered a Salt Lake City grocer. President Woodrow Wilson, World War I, and established labor unions killed the I.W.W.

Joyce L. Kornbluh, in her book REBEL VOICES, tells the story of the I.W.W.'s strikes, free-speech fights, trials and riots, militancy and martyrdom, sacrifices and oppression. She says of the Wobblies:

"They awakened the idealism and stirred the imagination of millions of workers. They laid the groundwork for the mass organization of the unskilled and foreign-born. They left their mark in the civil liberties field. . . . They stimulated investigations on the problems of migratory agricultural labor. Their agitations in jails against notorious prison abuses and use of prison contract labor led to public awareness which eventually brought about more humane conditions . . ."

They accomplished this in many ways, generally with the help of songs, usually written by Joe Hill.

The Wobblies protested the inhuman working conditions and restraints upon liberty that beset America just before World War I. Like the civil-rights workers of our time they stirred men and women to action by singing songs of freedom.

Woody Guthrie once remarked, "Leadbelly is the best living folk singer." After Leadbelly died, Pete Seeger said of him:

"He was not tall . . . but compactly built, and he moved with the soft grace of an athlete . . . he was gray-haired . . . always neatly dressed . . . always had a clean white shirt and starched collar, well-pressed suit and shined shoes . . . Looking back, I think that the most important thing I learned from him was the straight-forward approach, the direct honesty. He bequeathed to us also, it is true, a couple hundred of the best songs any of us will ever know."

The songs? Of those he gave to the world the most popular are *Rock Island Line; Goodnight, Irene; Old Cottonfields at Home; Take This Hammer; Leaving Blues; Pick a Bale o' Cotton; On a Monday; Boll Weevil; Black Girl; Midnight Special.*

The man? Woody has said, "You can go to the bookshelf and read his life from day unto day, I suppose, in more books than one." Here, briefly, are the facts and a few observations gleaned from the bookshelf.

Huddie Ledbetter was born into poverty around 1885 near Mooringsport, in the swamplands of Louisiana, not far from the Texas-Louisiana line; he died in poverty in New York City's Bellevue Hospital of amyotrophic lateral sclerosis—a disease of the muscles—on December 6, 1949.

Leadbelly was a born music maker, and at about two he could play the accordion. His life was a hard one. At first his father was a sharecropper, later a small farm holder (the crop was cotton), and as a young boy Leadbelly chopped and picked cotton. He rode a horse both to fetch provisions and to sing around the countryside at parties and square dances, where there was plenty of food, drink, and girls. Leadbelly was a father at sixteen. When the young woman had another child, not his, he left her.

For the next sixteen years he wandered, working and singing in many parts of the South. He picked cotton, sometimes more

RIGHT: *Huddie Ledbetter, the man known as "Leadbelly," died in 1949 just before his song* Goodnight, Irene *became a hit. He had learned the melody from an uncle some fifty-five years earlier on a farm in the Caddo Lake district. In addition to passing on traditional melodies, Leadbelly composed many of his own songs, which he performed while in prison in the South, in all manner of saloons and nightclubs, in recitals in Paris, and on the college circuit in the North. The* Harvard Crimson *in the nineteen-thirties summarized his importance when it said that he "brought a new kind of Negro music, a music of the Negro apart from his religion, simple and natural.... He played masterfully a twelve-string guitar, strumming violently as he sang in a deep rich voice tinged with the Louisiana dialect."*

than a bale a day—that is, five hundred pounds. He broke horses and worked at other odd jobs. Besides the accordion, he learned to play the double bass, the harmonica, the mandolin, the piano, and the six-, eight-, and twelve-string guitars. He learned songs while playing in saloons and on the streets of innumerable small towns and in cities, some as large as Dallas. For a while he accompanied Blind Lemon Jefferson, another exceptional Negro guitar player and singer.

In 1918 he was sent to a Texas prison farm to begin a thirty-year sentence for murder. He had been in a fight—a common enough occurrence in the hard life of the South—but this time a man died.

As a prisoner, Leadbelly worked hard and entertained well. The then governor of Texas visited the farm from time to time. Leadbelly tried singing for his freedom. He met with partial success.

Leadbelly is reported as quoting the governor's saying to him, "I'm gonna keep you down here to play for me when I come, but when I get outa this office, I'm gonna turn you loose if it's de last thing in the world I ever do." The governor kept his word: his successor pardoned Leadbelly in 1925.

Leadbelly went back to the life he led before being committed to the farm. Five years later, after fighting two other Negroes, he was convicted of assault with intent to kill and sent to a Louisiana penitentiary. It is said to have been a brutal place. Once again he appealed for clemency with a pardon song. It didn't work, because the governor had sworn never to pardon a prisoner. He was freed in August, 1934, before the end of his sentence because he had been a "good" prisoner.

Shortly afterward he went to work as John Lomax's chauffeur. Lomax and his son Alan, who traveled together through the South recording folk material, are described further in Chap. 8. With them Leadbelly toured Southern and Eastern universities. College students thought him marvelous.

In the North, he married Martha Promise from Shreveport, Louisiana, in January, 1935. The groom was fifty.

He became, for a short while, the center of considerable publicity and made the first of hundreds of recordings, which did not sell very well, broke with John Lomax, returned to Louisiana with Martha, then moved back to New York City, where he spent most of the rest of his life trying as best he could to make a living as a singer. Woody Guthrie recalls, "I've sung with Leadbelly in crazy painted rooms where I had to sit at a card table, draw losing hands, drink thirty-cent shots of hogwash, while Leadbelly sung in another room to make us a few cents to pay along towards the rent."

The trouble was that folk singing wasn't popular, not at least among any great number of people.

Occasionally, Josh White, who was doing well, invited Leadbelly to share the stage of Café Society in Greenwich Village. Josh White had also learned from blind, Southern rural singers— at the age of eight he began beating a tambourine and carrying a

Burl Ives began singing about the same time as Woody Guthrie and for a while they even traveled together. Besides touring internationally, performing on radio and TV, and appearing in Broadway musicals, he has also starred as a dramatic actor. Two of his important film appearances were in Cat on a Hot Tin Roof *and* East of Eden. *Like Harry Belafonte (now more a pop singer than a folk singer) and Josh White (also a polished stylist), Burl Ives has done much to bring folk singing to the attention of millions.*

tin cup. (There the similarity ends. Perhaps because he was born some thirty years after Leadbelly, Josh White had better chances at achieving success. In any case, he achieved it. He became a polished, theatrical-type entertainer, most popular in nightclubs during the forties. Significantly, he used his popularity to good purpose: he frequently sang such songs as *Strange Fruit* and *Jim Crow Train*—songs which protest racial injustice.)

Pete Seeger has written of Leadbelly:

"What a tragedy he died! It was just six months before his song *Goodnight, Irene* was selling two million copies, and making Hit Parade history. If he could have lived ten more years he would have seen all his dreams as a musician come true—young people by the millions learning and singing his songs. But in the nineteen thirties and forties the Hit Parade was dominated by the big bands, and all entertainment, to be successful, had to be geared to Hollywood standards. So Leadbelly sang for left-wing causes, Greenwich Village parties, and very occasional college concerts. We loved him, but I wish we hadn't been his only audience."

Today, Leadbelly albums include LEGACY, LEDBETTER'S BEST, and MIDNIGHT SPECIAL. The voice? A rough-hewn mansound rippled with the joy of living—with shouts, slurs, twangs, yells, and jazz rhythms.

There is no more hard traveling. Folk singers with any professional degree of talent and with any luck at all need no longer ride the rails, or sleep in parks, or panhandle. Just as significantly, folk singers are not pressed to the point of destruction if their political beliefs deviate from the majority view. The fact that in the mid-sixties many protest singers and other pop singers who draw heavily on the folk tradition are phenomenally successful is due in large measure to Joe Hill, Woody Guthrie, Leadbelly, and Pete Seeger, who created a good part of that tradition and who kept it alive when the traveling was indeed hard.

4 Sincerity and Swing

Frank Sinatra, who is about as far as you can get from a folk singer, nevertheless speaks for all singers who "feel" a song when he says:

". . . I get an audience involved, personally involved in a song —because I'm involved myself. It's not something I do deliberately; I can't help myself. If the song is a lament at the loss of love, I get an ache in my gut, I feel the loss myself and I cry out the loneliness, the hurt and the pain I feel. . . . Sentimentality, after all, is an emotion common to all humanity."

Some singers, though, go further than the Sinatra brand of sentimental empathy: Mahalia Jackson lives the life she sings about in her songs, while Joan Baez often uses songs to support causes she believes in.

For example, Joan Baez is against war, so she sings of her op-

position in Bob Dylan's *With God on Our Side*; she's against nuclear explosions and sings of her opposition in Malvina Reynolds'
What Have They Done to the Rain?

Now, a lot of people are against war, and only a few fanatics
call for dropping atomic or hydrogen bombs. Being for Peace is
almost as easy—when there isn't a war on—as being for God,
Mother, and Country. Expressing noble sentiments is the common
thing, is it not? Think of the preacher and the politician (often,
anyway), the butcher, the baker, and the schoolteacher. They are
all for the right thing. Talking is easy; doing's hard.

The thing about Joan Baez: she does.

In 1964 she refused to pay a large part of her income tax to
the United States Government. Internal Revenue agents were not
about to ignore her action; they took her house and land and car
and all her money in the banks of California. And they kept
charging her high interest as a penalty. An expensive business.

When asked why she had refused to pay, Joan Baez said that
she had been singing about banning the bomb and saying that she
didn't believe in organized murder and so forth and then at the
same time each year she was writing out a check to the Internal
Revenue Service. She said that it was false of her and so she decided to quit volunteering the money. It was a "symbolic protest,"
she said.

Symbolic protest: Not new and sometimes very effective.

An early symbolic protest was made in this country some hundred years ago when Henry Thoreau of Concord, Massachusetts,
went to jail for refusing to pay a tax to support the Mexican War.
When he emerged, after a friend paid his tax, he was so undis-

LEFT: *Joan Baez, the protesting pacifist who sings with a beautiful voice as
clear as sherry wine, has been described by Paul McCartney as "good, yeah,
very good."*

turbed that he went on a huckleberry-picking party. It was a jail term that never would have been remembered except for Thoreau's writing. He mentioned it in WALDEN (a book ". . . particularly addressed to poor students" not to accept the lives of quiet desperation led by "the mass of men") and in his essay *Civil Disobedience,* which contains the following passage:

"The night in prison was novel and interesting enough. The prisoners in their shirt-sleeves were enjoying a chat and the evening air in the doorway, when I entered. . . . The rooms were whitewashed once a month; and this one, at least, was the whitest, most simply furnished, and probably the neatest apartment in the town . . . I saw that if one stayed there long, his principal business would be to look out the window. I had soon read all the tracts that were left there, and examined where former prisoners had broken out, and where a grate had been sawed off, and heard the history of the various occupants of that room . . .

"Probably this is the only house in town where verses are composed, which are afterward printed in circular form, but not published. I was shown quite a long list of verses which were composed by some young men who had been detected in an attempt to escape, who avenged themselves by singing them."

This was certainly an early example of protest singing in America.

This essay inspired Gandhi, during India's revolution against the British Empire; and, later, Martin Luther King, in the civil rights movement; and, later still, Joan Baez, in her protest against nuclear weapons.

Although Joan Baez was not jailed, she did, no doubt, suffer for her actions. What must have hurt was the realization that she was doing something others—not *nice* people, anyway—wouldn't think of doing; that is, standing alone to say "No." It takes courage to set oneself aside in an unfavorable light, especially if you are almost certain that few will follow your example.

This exceptional young woman, one of three sisters, was born on Staten Island, New York, on January 9, 1941, during a period when her father, Dr. Albert Baez, was teaching at Wagner College. (Dr. Baez, born in Mexico and educated in the United States, has a Ph.D. in physics and is head of science teaching for UNESCO in Paris.)

Dr. and Mrs. Baez are Quakers. Joan Baez is not. She professes no formal religious affiliation; however, the Quaker influence no doubt accounts for her addressing the agents of the Internal Revenue Service as "Dear Friends."

She went to high school in Palo Alto, California, and attended Boston University's Fine Arts School of Drama for about a month. From time to time she has attended college classes—at Monterey Peninsula College, for example, and she runs an Institute for the Study of Nonviolence, in Menlo Park.

There is some talk that she sang rock 'n' roll before folk music; in any event, she has been known to sing rock 'n' roll since establishing her reputation. (She doesn't do it very well.)

Her first folk-song performances were in coffeehouses in Boston. In 1959, she and Bob Gibson—a writer-singer and twelve-string-guitar player of continuing influence—sang *Virgin Mary* and *Jordan River,* two traditional pieces, before an audience of thirteen thousand at Freebody Park in Newport, Rhode Island. The performance is reproduced as part of the album FOLK FESTIVAL AT NEWPORT, 1959, VOL. 2.

In 1960 Vanguard released her first album. By 1965 she had sold more LPs than any other woman folk singer, ever.

Joan Baez does not claim formal training of her voice.

She no longer sings in nightclubs or accepts engagements in coffeehouses. Most of her public singing is in concerts and in recording studios.

She is slender. Her hair is black and long, her face oval shaped, her eyes dark.

Her guitar playing is straightforward in style—a lilting, simple accompaniment to a full, firm, penetrating, often mournful and haunting voice. Once heard, it's a voice that I don't imagine can ever be forgotten. It's as clear as sherry wine and is beautifully feminine, like a mother crooning in a rocking chair.

More and more, Joan Baez is using her voice to sing songs that reflect what she deeply believes in, even as she continues to demonstrate her courage.

For example, the Pacifica Foundation, which owns and oper-

*More than any other singer,
Joan Baez has stood against
war and for civil rights.
Here she links arms with Bob
Dylan, the Freedom Singers,
Pete Seeger, and Peter,
Paul, and Mary during the
singing of* We Shall Overcome.

ates three listener-sponsored (noncommercial) radio stations (WBAI in New York, KPFA in Berkeley, and KPFK in Los Angeles), released an LP called IS FREEDOM ACADEMIC? On it are the voices of students, faculty, and sympathizers—and their opponents, the president and chancellor of the university. One of the voices of rebellion is that of Joan Baez, who leads the singing of *We Shall Overcome* and *Blowin' in the Wind* as one thousand students seize a campus building.

Besides presenting Joan Baez in direct action, the LP clarifies what actually happened at Berkeley in December, 1964, and for that reason belongs in the record library of every student concerned about civil liberties.

Briefly, what happened is that students seized the building and staged a sit-in, halting all campus activity, as part of a series of protests over a ban on fund-raising and recruiting on the campus for civil-rights demonstrations in the San Francisco Bay area. (At one rally for free speech and civil rights there were eleven thousand students out of the more than twenty-seven thousand enrolled.) To break up the sit-in, police arrested 814 demonstrators—all those who refused to leave after a warning—and dragged them off to jail. It was the biggest mass arrest in the United States since the Japanese (many of them American citizens) were hysterically rounded up in California early in World War II.

The LP also includes portions of a session of the faculty senate at which the faculty by a vote of eight to one sides with the students' cause.

IS FREEDOM ACADEMIC? presents an exceptional Baez performance. For typical Baez singing, listen to her own albums. The first of these, titled simply JOAN BAEZ, is made up of mostly traditional ballads—pretty, sad, and lonesome, but without much variety of sound or subject, though in *All My Trials* (a lullaby) she manages to project deep feeling and in *El Preso Numero Nueve* (a song in Spanish about a condemned prisoner who killed his wife and her lover) she provides the sort of change of pace that should have been interspersed throughout the album. There is no indication on this first album that one day Joan Baez would record protest songs.

JOAN BAEZ VOL. 2 is clearer and more powerful. Better programing, too. The songs, one to another, *sound* differently, but it's not until *Banks of the Ohio* and *Pal of Mine* that excitement cuts loose to gambol a while. Both tunes are backed up and pushed along by the Greenbriar Boys—of whom we'll hear more later. She's with them on *Pal of Mine*, and for the first time you can hear Joanie smile. For a moment the thought passes: She needn't be Joan of Arc, she could be a lovable little devil.

On JOAN BAEZ IN CONCERT, *Babe, I'm Gonna Leave You* is an example of what happens when a woman sings a song that should be sung by a man. No feeling. Another criticism I have is the way *Kumbaya*, a Negro gospel song, is presented. I don't like the audience participation. Although this is a ritual at folk concerts, and although a thousand voices can be exciting, they are often an in-

While thousands of university students crowd the front of a Berkeley, California, campus hall, police inside remove hundreds of "sit-ins." The day before (November 3, 1964), Joan Baez, in the vanguard of students protesting limitations on their political freedom, once again led in the singing of We Shall Overcome.

trusion—an omelet of sound. (Some of Pete Seeger's recorded concerts are exceptions.) I feel the same about the waves of clapping that follow each and every song on this album. Better that the metallic racket had been edited out.

Another performance flawed by group singing is recorded on JOAN BAEZ IN CONCERT PART 2. Joan Baez asks "Would you like to sing *We Shall Overcome?*" First, she hums a bit, then sings forth in an operatic voice which at times threatens to destroy her folk status. Meanwhile, way down is a muddle of sound—college students trying to sing along. One can see from the student rebellion at the University of California how *We Shall Overcome* (an adaption of an old Negro church song titled *I'll Overcome Someday*) is the song of our time. It is, however, best sung in connection with a demonstration, whether in a jail, on a picket line, or at a mass rally.

On JOAN BAEZ IN CONCERT is her first recorded performance of a protest song, *What Have They Done to the Rain?* The melody is beautiful, the words horrifying: "the boy disappears, and the rain keeps falling like helpless tears . . ." The musical pleasure and the editorial pain combine for an effect which is somewhat like that of drinking orange juice with a sizable dose of cod-liver oil. It's good for you, but the aftertaste is bittersweet.

The most moving of the protest songs she sings is on JOAN BAEZ/5. It is *Birmingham Sunday* by Richard Fariña. The poet Langston Hughes says in the album's notes:

". . . musically it is so beautifully understated . . . so softly sung . . . a quiet protest song . . . It was September 3, 1963, when four little girls went to Sunday School one Sabbath morning and never came back home. Instead they left their blood upon the church house wall, with spattered flesh and bloodied Sunday dresses torn to shreds by dynamite, victims of the race war in the American South."

As Paul McCartney puts it, "Joan Baez is good, yeah, very good." But, one thing about her; she doesn't swing. I sat through a jam-packed Baez concert in Newark, New Jersey, once; I didn't see a foot tap or a head bob. The music was pretty though, and there was enthusiastic applause after she sang, or when she made one of her cute quips.

One thing about Mahalia Jackson: she does swing. The Columbia album MAHALIA JACKSON: *The World's Greatest Gospel Singer* rocks and surges and thuds with beat and emotion. Mahalia sings Negro spirituals (which grew out of white Protestant hymns) such as *Keep Your Hand on the Plow,* and modern gospel songs like *I'm Going to Live the Life I Sing About in My Song.* The album also includes *I Will Move On Up a Little Higher*—a song she wrote herself and which as a single record sold over two million copies.

Mahalia Jackson, born in New Orleans in 1911, started singing at five in her father's church. (He worked during the week and preached on Sunday.) She never had a music lesson and still can't read music, but she heard the records made by the nonpareil blues singer Bessie Smith. At sixteen Mahalia moved to Chicago and began singing in the Greater Salem Baptist Church. She says:

"The true gospel song must retain the beat originally given it as a manifestation of religious happiness. The first gospels may have been the source from which the first jazz caught its beat . . . For me, there is a fundamental joy in everything I sing, 'cause I sing for the Lord."

The phenomena of foot tapping and head bobbing fascinate me. In New York City's Town Hall, the New Lost City Ramblers— three white musicians—stood rather stiffly on the stage and played Southern hillbilly, song after song of it. Town Hall was not jammed, but it was a good house. The audience were predominantly seventeen- and eighteen-year-olds. Mannered laughter, moderately enthusiastic clapping. Both performers and audience struck me as being only half with-it. I was reminded of one of

The church songs of Mahalia Jackson typify the rocking rhythms and surging lyrics of some folk music.

those devastating music-appreciation classes in high school or one of those cultural sessions—a museum lecture or a college assembly. But I wasn't there to hear the New Lost City Ramblers, anyway; I was waiting to listen to Elizabeth Cotten. A little, old colored lady—kind and dignified looking—came on the stage, was introduced, sat in a chair, and began playing a guitar. I had heard her before on the Folkways album, misspelled ELIZABETH COTTON. Her guitar playing is just beautiful, whether recorded or live. No rock, no bounce, but subtle rhythm patterns—a quiet jazz. Her singing sounds almost as if she isn't going to make it, but she always does. One can also hear a touch of laughter behind her unprofessional voice. Not since the early years of my bop listening has any musician compelled closer attention—the eyes-closed, head-bobbing kind.

But that Town Hall audience: I don't think they dug her. There was no visible or audible response except routine clapping after every song.

Elizabeth Cotten is a grandmother. She was born around the

turn of the century in Chapel Hill, North Carolina. In the forties she went to work as a maid in the Washington, D.C., household of Charles Seeger—Pete's father. There she heard Mike Seeger (Pete's half brother) practicing the guitar. Libba (her nickname) told him that at one time she played some, especially in her early teens. She played for him then and has played for many, many others since. Her finest contribution to our treasury of songs is one titled *Freight Train*.

It is hard to imagine voices sounding more different than do those of Elizabeth Cotten and Odetta—born Odetta Holmes, December 31, 1930, in Birmingham, Alabama.

First of all, there are physical differences: slight Elizabeth Cotten is a little, old lady: Odetta is a big (5′ 8½″), robust, young one; Elizabeth Cotten's voice is high, thin, and Sunday-summer-evening-on-the-front-porch sounding; Odetta's is deep, powerful, and Sunday-night-in-Carnegie-Hall sounding.

The biggest differences result from their backgrounds. Although both are Negroes, the older was raised in the Deep South, when only very few of her sex and race found opportunity beyond domestic work; the younger moved early in life to the West Coast,

Odetta, with a baritone voice of concert-hall magnitude and an innate sense of jazz, has invested folk music with unexcelled artistry. In sound and style Odetta is a world apart from Joan Baez— but like her, she is good, yeah, very good.

where she attended high school and university and where she formally studied voice.

Elizabeth Cotten is a folk singer; Odetta is a singer of folk songs. There will never be another Elizabeth Cotten. There will be many more Odetta-type singers, although they will have to be exceptionally talented to come up to her when she is at her best— for Odetta possesses one of the qualities of Elizabeth Cotten: a feeling for jazz. You can hear it on ODETTA SINGS FOLK SONGS.

Jazz in the form of the blues has been an important part of folk singing for some sixty years. Currently, this blues tradition is being passed from a dwindling number of old Negroes to a growing number of younger ones and to white singers, as well—especially in the exciting and popular music called folk-rock.

Elizabeth Cotten of North Carolina, creator of Freight Train, *plays and sings a quiet, beautiful jazz; stylistically she is a cousin to Mississippi John Hurt (see Chap. 5).*

5 Blues
and the Big Beat

Rock 'n' roll and its close cousin folk-rock owe much to jazz, to the blues, to hillbilly, and even to earlier British ballads. By the mid-sixties rock has become *the* popular music, virtually burying the Broadway musical-comedy songs, which were derived from the European operatic tradition. The songs of Irving Berlin, Richard Rodgers, Alan Jay Lerner and Frederic Loewe, and Frank Loesser are out (at least as far as single records are concerned); the songs of Ray Charles, Paul McCartney and John Lennon, Sonny Bono (of Sonny and Chér), and Bob Dylan are in. The changeover represents nothing less than a full-scale musical revolution. The old order of sweet-sounding sentimentality and artificial sophistications is over, replaced (when at its best) by shouting, crackling intensity and by intimate accounts of the pains and joys of real life today.

Although much of what the Beatles have been singing seems based on Elizabethan airs, the *sound* that they achieve (the Mersey sound) is no doubt the result of their having listened carefully to the American rock 'n' rollers: the Everly Brothers, Chuck Berry, and Little Richard. One might call this a sort of reverse lend-lease, but there is no cause for alarm or for legislation to stop the talent tap: in 1965, Dylan brought it all back home with folk-rock.

Shortly after Dylan's innovations, protest songs captured a large segment of the popular-record market. For example, the British singer Donovan (Leitch) made Buffy Sainte-Marie's *The Universal Soldier* a hit on both sides of the Atlantic, while Barry McGuire, a former member of the New Christy Minstrels, pushed P. F. Sloan's *Eve of Destruction* almost to the top of the record charts.

Of course, rock 'n' roll burst forth long before the Beatles or

Paul McCartney (left), a tunesmith, and John Lennon (right), a lyricist, create most of the Beatles' hits. They have been much influenced by folk songs of the Elizabethan Age and by rock 'n' roll of the nineteen-fifties.

Dylan. In the mid-fifties, Bill Haley and his Comets introduced rock 'n' roll with such hits as *Rock Around the Clock* and *See You Later, Alligator,* while Ray Charles fused blues, jazz, and gospel, and Elvis added a hillbilly flavor. All three were in turn influenced by the rhythm 'n' blues developed during World War II by singers like Big Bill Broonzy, who also sang country blues. It's a twisted path, but it can be followed by listening.

First of all, though, there is the confusing business of labels. Some sense can be made if one generalizes as follows: Hillbilly is white country music; rock 'n' roll is latter-day hillbilly plus rhythm 'n' blues, and rhythm 'n' blues is blues with a big beat.

And the blues, what are they?

The blues simply are songs that Negroes, mostly, have sung to keep on keeping on. Most often a blues is a cry, sometimes it is mocking laughter, sometimes, a sheer shout of courage.

"Consider some of the things the blues are about. They're about work, love, death, floods, lynchings; in fact a series of disasters which can be summed up under the arbitrary heading: 'Facts of Life.' " Thus James Baldwin on the blues. Another Negro novelist, the late Richard Wright, wrote:

"All American Negroes do not sing the blues. These songs are not the expression of the Negro people in America as a whole. I'd surmise that the spirituals, so dearly beloved of the Southern Whites, come from those slaves who were closest to the Big Houses of the plantations where they caught vestiges of Christianity whiffed to them from the Southern Whites' cruder forms of Baptist or Methodist religions. If the plantations' house slaves were somewhat remote from Christianity, the field slaves were almost completely beyond the pale. And it was from them and their descendants that the devil songs called the blues came . . ."

Besides reflecting the troubles and dreams of their creators, the blues reflect their talent for poetry. To appreciate just how much this is true, when you get a chance read THE POETRY OF THE BLUES, written by Samuel Charters and published by Oak; meanwhile, dig the following titles:

I'm a Steady Rollin' Man
On Our Turpentine Farm
Mosquito Moan
Big Leg Woman
Hard Times Ain't Gone Nowhere
Fattening Frogs
Standing By a Lamp Post
The Gone Dead Train
If I Could Holler
Chocolate to the Bone
River Hip Woman
You Got to Live and Let Live
I Ain't Gonna Be Your Fool
Dreamy-Eyed Woman's Blues
Baby, Quit Your Low Down Ways
Sissy Blues
Coon Can Shorty
The Sun Goes Down in Blood
Bring Me Flowers While I'm Living
Six Cold Feet in the Ground
See That My Grave Is Kept Clean
Mister Livingood
Hell Hound on My Trail
Money Green

At the beginning of this century Jelly Roll Morton played piano in New Orleans and sang *Winin' Boy Blues:* "Mama, mama, take a look at Sis/ Out on the levee, doin' the double twist." (Not only much of American singing, but also popular dancing comes straight from Southern Negro traditions.)

At about the same time, Leadbelly and Blind Lemon Jefferson were singing the blues in Texas.

Since then, Negroes have sung the blues North and South, in city and country, some (if their records sold) to wide acclaim.

Since the blues are for both singing and playing, various instruments are employed, depending on place of performance and style of performer.

Leadbelly, as mentioned earlier, played the accordion, the

double bass, the harmonica, the mandolin, the piano, and guitars of six, eight, and twelve strings. When he played at farm gatherings (picnics and dances) in Louisiana and East Texas jugs and washboards and fiddles were added.

As for the piano, it made popular not only Jelly Roll Morton's Spanish-tinged blues but also boogie-woogie—a hybrid form of the blues with eight beats to the bar. Rousing examples of boogie-woogie by Cripple Clarence Lofton (*Blue Boogie*), Pete Johnson

FAR LEFT: *Way-out costumed and long-haired Sonny and Chér, famous for* I Got You, Babe, *are folk-rockers who sing about the teenage scene.* LEFT, BELOW: *Ray Charles is a singing musician who combines blues, jazz, and gospel into an inimitable brand of rhythm 'n' blues, which he performs in a hoarse, growling, popping voice that sends audiences into happy frenzy.* LEFT: *Great-looking, blue-eyed Judy Collins, who began her career as a folk singer in the Joan Baez manner, has recently turned to singing the folk-rock of Bob Dylan.*   BELOW: *José Feliciano, a superb guitarist and an eclectic singer with a wide repertoire, now also sings folk-rock.*

(*Lone Star Blues*), and Jimmy Yancey (*The Fives*) are included in the RIVERSIDE HISTORY OF CLASSIC JAZZ.

But it is the guitar that has always been most popular among wandering singers of the blues. It is light, easily carried, and can be played loud enough to be heard in a crowded bar or over the din of a fast-rolling freight.

Besides portability and volume, there is another factor influencing choice of instrument, or instruments: the kind of blues.

There are three: **Classic, Country,** and **City.**

Classic Blues

The most popular time for the blues was in the twenties. As an aftermath of World War I, more and more Negroes were leaving the farms of the South for northern cities. By and large these colored migrants had enough trouble to want to hear the blues in order to "chase the blues away."

The first blues was recorded at the beginning of the decade by Mamie Smith, a vaudeville-style singer. The song she sang, *The Crazy Blues,* like most classic blues, was composed (in this case by Perry Bradford) but was delivered in the singer's own technique and tone. Classic-blues singers were professionals skilled in creating an aura of sophistication; they were, however, not proper ladies; in fact, they often got downright sexy with their dirty blues. As to this last point, Samuel Charters comments in THE POETRY OF THE BLUES:

"It is often in its colorful and elaborate sexual imagery that the blues is most vividly poetic. There is a sauntering flamboyancy to the language, a sudden image in one verse crowding into the next, its intended effect broadened with the tone of the voice or the rhythm of the guitar or the piano. An exuberant, gusty delight in sexuality is expressed in an imagery which still has the vigor and freshness of its folk roots. Instead of the reticence or the leering innuendo of American popular song there is in the blues an open acceptance of the pleasure of sexual love."

At recording sessions, classic-blues singers were usually backed up by jazz musicians—the barrelhouse players. The result: swinging, gutty records that are marvelous to listen to even now and that back in the twenties were bought for seventy-five cents each, at the rate of five million a year. (Bessie Smith, as Columbia Records' biggest artist, was responsible for saving that company from bankruptcy; in 1924, sales of her records exceeded two million copies, and for a time she was making $1,500 a week.)

Most of the classic-blues singers were women. Besides Bessie, among the most prominent were Ma Rainey, Ida Cox, Memphis Minnie, Merline Johnson, Victoria Spiney, and Lil Green. Because the discs they recorded were sold exclusively in Negro communities they were called "race records." These, like all the records of the time, were made of shellac and played with a steel needle suspended from the heavy arm of a Victrola whose 78-rpm turntable was set spinning by means of a hand crank (Lo-Fi).

Shack town in Philadelphia, Mississippi, where men, women, and children have every reason to cry the blues.

Bessie Smith was the most celebrated classic-blues singer, while the most celebrated song has been *St. Louis Blues,* composed by W. C. Handy. Handy was called the "Father of the Blues" because he was the first to publish and copyright a blues tune—*Mamie's Blues,* in 1909.

An excellent recording of classic blues is Volume I of a four-volume set titled THE BESSIE SMITH STORY. On it Bessie sings ten songs, seven of them to the cornet accompaniment of Louis Armstrong—the great man of jazz. One of the seven is *St. Louis Blues* —the classic blues' classic performance. To hear Louis himself singing the blues, listen to LOUIS ARMSTRONG PLAYS W. C. HANDY.

At the height of the Roaring Twenties, record companies sent scouts with microphones into Negro sections of the big towns— Atlanta, Houston, Jackson, Kansas City, Memphis, New Orleans, St. Louis, Vicksburg, and so forth—and into the rural hamlets of the Carolinas, Georgia, Mississippi, Tennessee, and Texas. The scouts searched out and recorded performances by city-blues and country-blues singers. Many of these recordings were added to the companies' race-record catalogs. With the start in 1929 of the Great Depression, the boom in race records—as the boom in real estate, stocks, and everything else—ended. The whole nation should have taken up listening to blues singers, but the whites hardly knew they existed, and not many Negroes had seventy-five cents to spare for a piece of shellac, no matter how crazy the cut.

Country Blues

The Mississippi Delta is a land of blues, cotton, and murder. Julius Lester, who spent part of the summer of 1964 there with the Caravan of Music, expresses all three, playing bottleneck style and singing with haunting deep feeling, in his *Delta Blues:* "It's down in the Delta/ Cotton up to my door."

Julius Lester is dedicated to preserving the heritage of his people. He does so by composing and singing blues songs and by contributing articles to Sing Out! *magazine.*

And he introduces a song titled *Dead and Gone* by recalling an incident in which half a human body and parts of another were hooked by a fisherman on the Pearl River, which separates Mississippi and Louisiana. Although the streams and rivers of Mississippi served as a regular dumping ground for murdered and lynched Negroes, interest was aroused by the fisherman's discovery, because, says Julius Lester, the search was on for three missing Mississippi civil-rights workers—two of whom were white.

However, the interest quickly waned when it was discovered that the remains were not those sought, but just part of the regular toll.

Julius Lester sings:

> Poor boy, dead and gone.
> Lord, he's lyin' in his grave,
> Never did a damn thing wrong.
> I asked the Lord
> Don't let Pearl River
> Be my burying ground.

Lester's performance in January, 1965, at the earlier mentioned *Broadside* Hootenanny in Greenwich Village was part of the country-blues revival which began during the late fifties.

The most significant event in this revival, as far as male singers are concerned, occurred just the year before Lester's performance when a seventy-two-year-old man—with a farm-worn face, and a singing and playing style virtually unheard—was rediscovered in Avalon, Mississippi (a hamlet with a population of two hundred in the hill country at the edge of the Delta).

Mississippi John Hurt, who made a reputation as a blues singer back in 1928 when he recorded for OKeh label, was rediscovered in 1963 and propelled into the forefront of the folk-song revival.

Rediscovered? It's a word representing a peculiar concept, as does the word *discovery* when used, say in connection with a place such as America (Indians, had they been informed, would have been quite perplexed to learn of Columbus' feat).

What does it mean to say that John Hurt of Avalon was rediscovered? He wasn't lost—not to his wife, his friends, his employer. Had never been, in fact. It means simply that John Hurt, once discovered by a white man looking for records to make back in the twenties, was rediscovered by another white man with the same purpose in the sixties. This latter event was reported, in due course, by *Down Beat,* the *Little Sandy Review, The New York Times, Sing Out!* and *Time* for the enlightenment of folk-music lovers.

Rediscovery—peculiar terminology, perhaps, but as an event and a process it is not to be put down; for it has meant a lot to Mississippi John—who now has a wide audience and who no longer farm-labors for twenty-eight dollars a month. To *Discoverer* Tom Hoskins, a blues collector of Washington, D.C., goes the credit for bringing back to large numbers of Americans a forgotten style of country music that, not so much bluesy as rag-timey, enriches all those who can and will appreciate singing and playing that is subtle, pulsating and warm. Stylistically, Mississippi John is a cousin to that other discovery, mentioned earlier, Elizabeth Cotten.

Unlike John Hurt, those singers who actually grew up in the main part of the Delta sting with their blues, evoking a sense of intensely felt dramatic emotions. One accepts that they feel deeply, even if one doesn't share the feeling. Big Joe Williams, who was born in the heart of the Delta in 1899 and who now lives in Chicago, is an excellent representative of the style. MISSISSIPPI BIG JOE WILLIAMS AND HIS NINE-STRING GUITAR is a good example of his work—singing and playing that now has appeal to only a limited audience.

The year before the world again heard from Mississippi John Hurt, a documentary film maker took a photograph of Sleepy John Estes at his tumbledown sharecropper's shack outside Brownsville, Tennessee. Now Sleepy John has admiring listeners, just as he did almost forty years ago.

Today, country-blues singing is not very popular, no matter who sings, be it Big Joe Williams or Sleepy John Estes. Sleepy John is another rediscovery, lost for two decades. In 1962, he was found for the second time, blind and living with his wife and family in a squalid shack in Brownsville, Tennessee. Since then he has been recorded again and presented at folk festivals and such coffeehouses as Chicago's old Fickle Pickle. Times are better for him, but the blues he sings are, for most, just an oddity.

City Blues

Not only country-blues singers have had hard times for the last two decades; so also have those bluesmen who sang a message meaningful to their fellows in the twenties and the thirties—a message that relieved the tensions of life in the city ghettos, as the country-blues relieved it in the land of cotton.

The city bluesmen are countless (mostly because new legendary names keep popping up in record columns). In any case, there is little point in compiling a list, for, except musicologists, hardly anybody really cares any more. John Lee Hooker, originally of Memphis, now of Detroit, and Sam "Lightnin' " Hopkins of Houston, Texas (he *studied* under Blind Lemon Jefferson), get some attention when they sing the old songs in the old style, but the attention is from those who love the old for the old's sake.

They get more enthusiastic receptions when they sing rhythm 'n' blues in a style developed during World War II. The interesting thing is that just like Big Bill Broonzy they can perform in both styles—piercing city blues, to the accompaniment of a guitar, and rhythm 'n' blues, to wailing saxes and driving drums along with electrically amplified guitars. A good example of both styles on the same album is BIG BILL BROONZY MEMORIAL.

The words are pretty much the same, whether city blues or rhythm 'n' blues. The difference is in the beat. Rhythm 'n' blues performances I especially like are on the albums JIMMY WITHERSPOON AT THE MONTEREY JAZZ FESTIVAL and AMERICAN FOLK BLUES FESTIVAL. Performers on the latter are Memphis Slim, Sonny Terry, Brownie McGhee, T-Bone Walker, John Lee Hooker, Shaky Jake, Jump Jackson, and Willie Dixon. The album was recorded at a wildly enthusiastic concert in Hamburg, Germany.

Both are good albums but they never became best sellers. Raw rhythm 'n' blues, as played by Muddy Waters, is a driving, rocking, honking, bleating music, sometimes described as having a funky sound. It's too strong for general tastes. Even among younger Negroes it's falling from favor. However, white folk enthusiasts are taking it up. Herein lies a paradox: when a musical style loses meaning among audiences for whose enjoyment or enrichment it was originally created, it becomes folk music.

One of the strangest variations of this paradox began to occur in the sixties: white citybillies were trying to sing the blues as if they were Negro bluesmen. A representative sample of citybillies is recorded on BLUES PROJECT. They are Dave Van Ronk, John

Koerner, Geoff Muldour, Dave Roy, Danny Kalb, Ian Buchanan, Mark Spoelstra, and Eric Von Schmidt. Others of this type who have achieved some attention on records and in clubs include John Hammond (son of the record producer mentioned in Chap. 2) and Paul Butterfield. (For the blues singing of a white woman who preceded the citybillies by some five years, hear BARBARA DANE SINGS THE BLUES.)

The phenomenon of middle-class white, college-educated (at least a few years of college, anyhow) young men trying to sound like poverty-stricken, oppressed Negroes is very ironic for two reasons:

1. It is virtually impossible for a white man to cry the blues the way a Negro does. Crying is largely a reflex reaction: one doesn't choose to weep; one can't help oneself. And few white men have lived long enough among segregated Negroes to really feel their pain. (One who did is novelist Warren Miller who wrote THE COOL WORLD after living five years in Harlem.) Also, middle-class whites have never had to wander to look for work, they have never had to go without adequate food, and they have never had to fear the police because of their social or economic position.

2. For almost all Negro professional singers, the old-style blues have become irrelevant to their lives.

It's silly, then, for young whites to try to feel and express, through songs, what they cannot know and what Negroes themselves no longer feel or express.

While white singers of the blues chase ghosts, Negroes keep investing their blues' inheritance in American popular music. For examples, there are the albums of Ray Charles (THE GENIUS SINGS THE BLUES) and B. B. King (THE BLUES)—two mature

---

LEFT: *The Paul Butterfield Blues Band stacks up on a tenement stairs in Chicago's South Side. When they blast forth, their bluesy folk-rock harmonica and guitars are wired for sound. Boys in foreground symbolize the fact that the band draws heavily on Negro-created rhythm 'n' blues.*

artists—and the singles of the late thirty-three-year-old Sam Cooke. Interestingly, Cooke, a big-beat rock 'n' roll singer, was steeped in spirituals by his father, a Baptist minister.

Moreover, the big-beat tradition is being picked up by very young Negroes. A case in point is the recording activity of the Negro-owned-and-operated company Motown, located in a Detroit enclave happily nicknamed "Hitsville U.S.A." In the sixties, Motown released records by young colored singers, including the Supremes, three women in their early twenties. Motown falls mostly in a category called the "Detroit Sound."

Ray Charles has said, "At one time rhythm 'n' blues was nothing; then all of a sudden along came a *Blue Suede Shoes* and one or two others; then it became rock 'n' roll, and it was a big thing."

Yes, a big thing. It has been so since Elvis began blasting and wiggling to create a new musical era not only in America but in Africa, Communist China, Europe, India, Japan, the Near East, the Soviet Union—everywhere. He possesses that mysterious

When curly-lashed, baby-mouthed Elvis appeared on the "Ed Sullivan Show" in 1956 the cameras concentrated on his face—his body gyrations would have brought screams of protest from parents. *Within a few years, however, men and women of almost all ages were twisting away. But Elvis' biggest contribution to popular culture has been the singing style known as "rockabilly"—a synthesis of country-and-western and rhythm 'n' blues.*

charismatic gift of audio presence, and his records have been bought in greater quantities than those of any other singer except Bing Crosby—who has been making his for forty years. (To recapture the style of the mid-fifties Elvis, listen to the first LP in Victor's ELVIS' GOLDEN RECORDS series. It includes *Hound Dog, Heartbreak Hotel, Don't Be Cruel.*)

Elvis and the Beatles and the Rolling Stones, the Dave Clark Five, the Righteous Brothers, the Supremes, Mary Wells, Sonny and Chér, and Bob Dylan, and so forth—all add up to a groovy scene without comparable precedent. Certainly Rock surpasses Swing. Swing lasted for a shorter time—1936 into World War II—still it has much in common with Rock, at least as far as enthusiasm goes. In I LIKE JAZZ, I wrote:

"Kids then, parents today. Now they might try to show their vigor by shaking to the latest dance craze; in those days there was no need to prove they could get *with* it. As time neared for the start of one of the dance-band radio broadcasts, rugs were rolled up in living rooms throughout the country, and when the band cut loose with a hot number, bobby-soxer and zoot-suiter launched into the jitterbug. The fuddy-duddies viewed with alarm, and nagged about adolescent naughtiness. But whether or not their parents liked it, when Swing came out of a loudspeaker, kids had fun."

Now of parental age, some of those fans have intellectualized the kicks they got then, and when they relisten to Swing they claim that it is the true classic jazz music. I believe the pattern will repeat itself: today's kids will grow old and, sometime in the next twenty years, the durable appreciators among their number will be writing essays and delivering lectures praising rock 'n' roll as America's most pervasive contribution to the musical culture of the world. Yes, I'm willing to bet that's what will happen. But whether it actually does or not doesn't really matter. What counts is enjoying now the most exciting singing style in America, ever!

6 Blue Grass, Country-and-Western, Old Timey— by any name, it's Hillbilly

One type of blues, at least a blues in name, the talking blues, comes from the Negroes ("There ain't no use of me workin' so hard/ I got a woman in the white folks' yard"), but the form has been taken over and elaborated upon by white singers (Bob Dylan, Phil Ochs, and others) in the sixties. The talking blues is usually performed—to guitar accompaniment—in a deadpan style with punch lines thrown off the strict 4/4 time to achieve a maximum humorous (often satirical) effect on an audience. Most talking blues since the thirties have been protest songs —complaints about unemployment, labor-union busting, bad working conditions, and war ("So listen folks, here's my thesis:/ Peace in the world, or the world in pieces" are the key lines from *Old Man Atom,* composed in 1946 by Vern Partlow). The most famous talking blues are the work of Woody Guthrie. Some of these, along with the works of others, can be heard, sung by John Greenway, on TALKING BLUES.

There is yet another type of blues that when sung by whites turns out not to be blues at all.

Woody Guthrie on side four of the LIBRARY OF CONGRESS RECORDINGS sings *Worried Man Blues* ("It takes a worried man to sing a worried song") and then explains that it is not blues but a lament, with a "churchouse blues" lick to it. He says he first heard it sung by the Carter family.

A. P. Carter, a fruit-tree salesman; Sara Daugherty Carter, courted after A. P. met her on his sales rounds; and Maybelle Carter, A. P.'s sister-in-law, were churchouse-blues singers from Rye Cove, Virginia, in the Southern Appalachian Mountains. They began recording in August, 1927, for RCA Victor and within a few years had sold more than ten million records. Among some of the songs they helped make famous are *The Foggy Mountain Top, God Gave Noah the Rainbow Sign, Little Moses,* and *Jimmie Brown, the Newsboy.* Carter Family songs were, for the most part, traditional Anglo-Saxon ballads and white spirituals with revised lyrics and with melodies adapted for accompaniment by guitar and autoharp, or Negro songs, similarly revised. *Worried Man Blues,* for example, was arranged by A. P. after he heard it sung by a convict labor gang.

The original Carter Family disbanded in 1943—having recorded almost three hundred songs.

Other groups that recorded rural music in the twenties and thirties include the Monroe Brothers, from western Kentucky, and the Dixon Brothers, from Darlington County, South Carolina. They are among the artists presented on SMOKY MOUNTAIN BALLADS, an excellent, happy sample of early hillbilly. Uncle Dave Macon of Tennessee is also on the album. He was one of the earliest "Grand Ole Opry" performers. Appearing as "The

Dixie Dewdrop" and "The King of the Hillbillies," he was famous from the late twenties to the early forties for "handling a banjo like a monkey handles a peanut."

To a large extent, the modern history of hillbilly is the history of the Grand Ole Opry and the station which has broadcast it, WSM of Nashville, Tennessee.

The program began as the "WSM Barn Dance" in 1925 with Uncle Jimmy Thompson, then in his eighties, who boasted that he could "fiddle the bugs off a sweet potato vine." Since then, Ryman Auditorium, home of the Grand Ole Opry, has been filled every Saturday night for 270 minutes with the sound of nasal twangs, lusty yodels, plaintive cries, the thumping of tubs, the blowing of jugs, the strumming and picking of guitars and banjos, the scraping of fiddles, the stomping of dancing feet, and the clapping of hands by thousands of listeners.

The show is heard by millions, many of whom listen to it rebroadcast from tape segments of an hour's duration—generally played five days a week—over some four hundred radio stations. Other millions watch the show over television.

Nashville is to hillbilly what Hollywood was to the movies in its heyday. As with Hollywood, Nashville's importance is that it is *the* center of talent (performers on the Grand Ole Opry) and of technical skills (recording studio engineers). Largely, since the Elvis Revolution, Nashville's talents and technicians have been creating a music described as having the "Nashville Sound." It is a *big* sound: lots of singers supported by lots of electric-guitar players, all *coordinated* by electronic editors who *doctor up* tapes until they meet the standards of a salable product. This product, sometimes called "rockabilly," is part of the country-and-western tradition—the folk music of the Electronic Age. Its most popular singers include Johnny Cash, Jimmy Dean, Lefty Frizzell, Roger Miller, and Marty Robbins.

American country-and-western, descended from the centuries-

old music of Scotland and Wales, was developed by the mountain people of the American South and the plainsmen of the West.
Not until the introduction of radio, however, did it become, in
various forms, a mass entertainment.

"One of the strongest and most easily traced threads of the
purer vocal and instrumental tradition which still thrives in the
midst of the Nashville potpourri is the segment of country music
now known as 'blue grass.' " Thus writes Ralph Rinzler in the
notes to an excellent introduction to blue grass, THE GREENBRIAR
BOYS album.

(The Greenbriar Boys won the Old-Time Band Competition
at the Fiddler's Convention in Union Grove, North Carolina, in
1960 and, two years later, appeared on Grand Ole Opry, making
them the first northern group to play the radio station in twenty-
five years.)

Rinzler states:

"[The name blue grass] came into being along with the work
of the dynamic figure who was the main-spring of the music itself.
This was Bill Monroe, a powerful tenor singer and mandolin
virtuoso of the highest caliber, who joined Grand Ole Opry in
October, 1939, and performed with his band called the Blue
Grass Boys. [Monroe's album KNEE DEEP IN BLUE GRASS is a
classic.] In the forties and fifties most of the new stars . . . went
through a period of apprenticeship with Monroe by traveling and
performing with him. [Some of the characteristics of blue grass
are] the presence of virtuoso instrumentalists, the almost total
absence of electrically amplified instruments, the vocal treatment
which usually features a prominent tenor voice in a duet, trio or
quartet combination, the inclusion of wholly traditional songs,
ballads and hymns in the repertoire and the exclusive use of string
instruments. These are principally the guitar, fiddle, banjo, mandolin, dobro (non-electrified Hawaiian steel) on occasion, and
plucked string bass for accompaniment."

Flatt and Scruggs got their start with the Grand Ole Opry and certified their talent by playing Carnegie Hall. Lester Flatt, a tenor, is the lead singer for their band and Earl Scruggs is the man who revolutionized the playing of the five-string banjo. They play hillbilly music that is palatable even to city slickers.

Among the outstanding performers associated with Bill Monroe are Earl Scruggs, the fastest banjo picker in the world, who has also been described as making "folk music in overdrive, with a silvery, rippling pinging sound," and Lester Flatt, a guitarist and lead singer. In 1945, Earl Scruggs' three-fingered picking style with its continuous flow of notes from his five-string banjo was heard for the first time on the Grand Ole Opry. In 1948 Flatt and Scruggs formed their own band, the Foggy Mountain Boys. In 1962 their single record *Ballad of Jed Clampett* was the number-one seller among country-and-western records, and, in the same year, they appeared in concert at Carnegie Hall. In reporting on the concert, reviewer Charles Sinclair said of Lester Flatt, the group's master of ceremonies, that "he sported a Texas-styled hat, a bright red bow tie and the kind of suit that might be worn by a prosperous Nashville dentist" and that "he joshed the audience, between numbers, with such mountain-grown gassers as 'This here's Uncle Jake Tullock on the bass. His ma and pa are well off—in fact his whole family's a bit *off*!'" Sinclair said that the four members of the group backing the headliners did so with the "polished precision of the Budapest String Quartet." Reviewers often get carried to the heights of hyperbole when discussing the Foggy Mountain Boys; Robert Shelton, for example, said that "Earl Scruggs bears about the same relationship to the five-string banjo that Paganini does to the violin."

Be that as it may, the evening was recorded and released on the exciting album FLATT AND SCRUGGS AT CARNEGIE HALL. Listen also to FOGGY MOUNTAIN BANJO, a sparkling collection of Flatt, Scruggs, and their band, playing traditional blue-grass instrumentals.

Another happy album of Southern sounds is OLD TIME MUSIC AT CLARENCE ASHLEY'S, with songs, including *Sally Ann, Old Ruben,* and *Footprints in the Snow,* performed by Ashley and eight other musicians who live in the mountain-country towns of Saltville, Virginia; Pilot Mountain and Deep Gap, North Carolina; and Shouns, Tennessee. Ralph Rinzler, joined by Richard Rinzler, in the notes to the album explains:

"Before the era of the Opry and phonograph records, medicine shows and circuses were the main sources of entertainment in rural areas, and as a variety of attractions was the general rule in these shows, music was supplied by anywhere from one performer, in a small off-season medicine show, to four or five singers and instrumentalists in a large summer company. Like Fiddling John Carson [the first recorded hillbilly performer] and Uncle Dave Macon . . . Ashley travelled the medicine show circuits in the early days; he picked the banjo, sang ballads and comic songs, told funny stories and did his share of chores. Starting out as a musician at the age of sixteen, he continued to travel the country-side alone and with various groups until very recently."

The album presents seventeen songs representing the musical life of a man who was seventy-five years old in 1965. Doc Watson, the blind, white guitar player from Deep Gap, who is one of the performers on the Ashley album, has become famous in his own right among old-time-music enthusiasts.

The already mentioned New Lost City Ramblers have done much to cull from the thousands of hillbilly records of the late twenties and thirties those songs and those styles which interest northern city audiences who find in old-time music's robust frontier rhythms a quaint change from the popular Tin Pan Alley product.

In 1965 the New Lost City Ramblers were Mike Seeger, John Cohen, and Tracy Schwarz—the latter having replaced Tom Paley in 1963. Seeger and Cohen are the editors of the NEW LOST CITY RAMBLERS SONG BOOK (125 songs plus prefatory essays). Cohen is also a film maker and photographer, while Mike Seeger searches out old-time performers on their home grounds. In this role, Mike Seeger discovered Dock Boggs, a long-lost Kentucky banjo player. Boggs, who recorded in the late twenties, became an object of interest among folklorists in the forties and then a legend because, ironically, they couldn't find out anything about him; in the sixties, Mike Seeger, spotting his name in a Norton, Virginia, phone book, gave Boggs a call and discovered him to be a retired coal miner still playing and singing in his community.

There are many, many hillbilly singers. There are authentic ones who appeal to the aficionados of the folk tradition: The most famous, Frank Proffitt, died in November 1965, at his home in Beaver Dam—a tiny farm community in the southern Appalachians. He was of great importance because he preserved traditional mountain ballads, which he sang in a flat, coarse, drowsy voice, and because he carried on a venerable craft of making banjos by hand. He acquired national attention when *Tom Dulla,* a song passed to him by his father, became a jukebox hit sung by the Kingston Trio under the title *Tom Dooley.* Other authentics include Roscoe Holcomb and Wade Ward, expert banjoists and singers who have also traveled the festival circuit; and Jean Ritchie, who, born in Kentucky, has carried beautiful ballads and lonesome love songs (preserved by her family) and the sound

Roscoe Holcomb, a farmer and construction worker from Daisy, Kentucky, has sung old ballads and Baptist hymns, with a nasal twang characteristic of the hillbilly, at all major festivals from Berkeley to Brandeis.

of the dulcimer all over the United States, Canada, and Europe. Then there are two hillbillies who once had a fantastic effect on the popular culture of both the United States and large parts of the rest of the world.

Jimmie Rodgers, born in Meridian, Mississippi, in 1897, wrote and recorded, and sang in a high-pitched voice, more than a hundred songs from August 4, 1927, to May 24, 1933—two days before he died of tuberculosis. Known variously as the "Singing Brakeman" and the "Father of the Country Field," he was honored three decades after his death as the first member of the Country Music Hall of Fame. Rodgers, in singing his blue yodels, combined white mountain ballads and Negro blues in a way that entertained millions of people and for some reason satisfied their emotional needs. RCA Victor has issued a series of albums of his songs, including COUNTRY MUSIC HALL OF FAME.

The other great name in the modern hillbilly field is Hank Williams. The hillbilly Shakespeare began recording in 1948 and until his death at the age of twenty-nine, of a heart attack on New Year's Day, 1953, wrote and sang weepers, novelties, and sacred songs. Some of the hits he contributed to American popular entertainment include *I Just Don't Like This Kind of Livin',* *Cold, Cold Heart, Hey Good Lookin', Jambalaya,* and *Your Cheatin' Heart.*

Hank Williams sang for the folks just like that other *hillbilly* Woody Guthrie, but there is a world of difference in how they sang and what they sang about. It's a difference worth listening to and pondering.

7 Groups and the Big Time

Words aren't much help in defining styles of sound, whether they be the New Thing, Third Stream, Neo-Bop, Cool, Dixieland, Swing, and so forth of jazz; or the citybilly, hillbilly, and rock 'n' roll of folk. Even WEBSTER'S NEW INTERNATIONAL DICTIONARY hedges over rock 'n' roll by defining it as "jazz characterized by a strong beat and much repetition of simple phrases often with both blues and folk song elements." (WEBSTER'S doesn't list rhythm 'n' blues at all.)

If dictionaries evade the issue, one can't expect musicians or authors to be much bolder. Big Bill Broonzy, for example, mocked the problem by saying, "I guess all songs is folk songs. I never heard no horse sing 'em."

The only way out of the labyrinth of labels is to follow a subtle guide known as taste—the supreme arbiter because every person can make it serve his or her own needs. I remember an old adage (at least, old to me—since my father used it often to quiet a son eager to get problems in their proper pigeonholes): "Son," he'd say, "remember what the old woman answered when asked why she kissed the cow? 'Everyone to their own taste.'" Not grammatical, but wise—and applicable to styles of singing in contemporary America.

If you favor the New Christy Minstrels with your attention, you are not too far from Mitch Miller and his sing-along society. To my taste neither group is worth the time spent listening. Their singing is pap-pop to me—although I wouldn't be a bit surprised if one found, without much of a search, somebody claiming the Minstrels a folk group or crediting Mitch Miller with reviving the folk tradition.

Peter, Paul and Mary (two beards and a blonde) are current folk-song favorites among the college aged.

If, on the other hand, you like to listen to Peter, Paul, and Mary, you're closer to my taste. Yet, here again, the labyrinth of labels. One would think Peter, Paul, and Mary a folk group, what with their guitars and their songs from Bob Dylan, Elizabeth Cotten, Woody Guthrie, and all, but surprise! they show up year after year as vocal-group winners of *Playboy* magazine's All-Star Jazz Band poll. Wow! Peter, Paul, and Mary—without drums, without saxophones, without piano—jazz makers?

Be they folk or jazz, Peter, Paul, and Mary are compelling entertainers, especially on their album IN THE WIND. They've been appealing from their beginning—from the time they went public after Albert Grossman, their manager, put them together. It's said he went searching for "two beards and a blonde" after he detected an opening in the market at the demise of the original Kingston Trio.

When the Kingston Trio was Nick Reynolds, Bob Shane, and Dave Guard, it held sway over the folk-pop market from 1957— the year of *Tom Dooley*—to 1961. After pocketing royalties from some three million copies of *Tom Dooley* alone, they just didn't think working together was worth the difficulties they had in getting along.

The fact is that folk-pop singing groups are not motivated by a desire to create lasting art. Neither are they out to entertain their friends, nor do they sing to help themselves through a dull, exhausting job of work—two reasons old-time folks sang traditional songs. No, folk-poppers sing for money and they are successful only when they earn it. What determines this success is the subject of the following analysis by Francis Newton in *The New Statesman*:

"They [the people] will welcome the products of such folk traditions as have shown themselves capable of surviving into industrial society, which does not mean weavers' songs and sea chanties, but rhythm 'n' blues, country-and-western, and some

The current Kingston Trio (left to right, John Stewart, a former rock 'n' roll singer, Bob Shane, and Nick Reynolds), is a commercially oriented act famous for such songs as Desert Pete. *In 1957 the original Kingston Trio (Dave Guard instead of John Stewart) brought folk music to unprecedented popularity with the song* Tom Dooley.

jazz. This living tradition is no longer amateur but professional and commercial, and it has been musically transformed by street-song, vaudeville numbers and increasing pop influences. But the fact that we may prefer something more antique doesn't make the hillbilly professionals and urban Negro rockers any less folky. The public will accept, and welcome, good folk tunes from the traditional repertoire, if they fit its taste . . . If the folk movement is genuinely to reach the folk, it must therefore be prepared to see its material absorbed by commercialism."

Absorbed it has been. Just how deeply is a point emphasized by *Billboard,* the international music-record newsweekly, in this spirited review of a Peter, Paul, and Mary performance:

"In a sold-out concert at Carnegie Hall, the folk-oriented trio exhibited the kind of successful slickness one associates with the big Detroit motor makers. The group's performance was as shiny as new chromium, as glossy as a two-tone hardtop, and as commercial as a convention of credit managers.

"In short, Peter, Paul, and Mary have about the same relationship to genuine American folk singing as a four-seater Thunderbird has to a classic Ferrari racing car. The PP&M product is designed for popular easy consumption with just enough nonconformity thrown in to make the purchaser feel that he's one-up on the common herd although purists wouldn't be caught dead near it. However, a lot more Thunderbirds than Ferraris are sold, purists notwithstanding.

"PP&M put on a good show, and they're certainly one of the country's top folk acts by any standard. Many of their Carnegie numbers—*The Lemon Tree, Flora, the Lily of the West, Where Have All the Flowers Gone?, I Wish I Was a Single Girl*— were from recent LPs or from their regular concert repertoire, and have drive, pace and polish. The show's audience, most of whom seemed to be Ivy college types . . . ate it up, with particularly strong applause reserved for the group's best-known record hits.

"Like other top folk groups, PP&M have learned how to strike just the right balance of collegiate erudition and blue-grass folksiness, a trick which can often be seen at work in the introductions to vocal numbers. Paul, the group's tall, bearded spokesman, never simply brings on a song with 'And now, for our next number, we'd like to play for you . . . etc.' In his introduction to the

Irish oldie, *There's Whisky in the Jar* Paul referred to it as 'a song of social protest, in the same way that LADY CHATTERLEY'S LOVER is a social protest.' It wowed the collegians."

To a lesser extent, the collegians have been wowed by a raft of other groups: the already mentioned Kingston Trio, the Mitchell Trio, the Clancy Brothers and Tommy Makem (four Irishmen), Ian and Sylvia (two Canadians), the Limeliters, the Roof Top Singers, the Journeymen, the Brothers Four, the Smothers Brothers, and so on.

The Weavers were once *the* group. They too were commercial. They came early in the folk revival, they were older in age than the largely collegiate groups, and they had personal ties with the folk singing of the thirties and forties and especially with Woody Guthrie. During their fifteen years, they were the standard in folk music.

Pete Seeger, Lee Hays, Fred Hellerman, and Ronnie Gilbert made their professional debut in 1948 at the Village Vanguard in New York City. In 1950 they had two hit songs: *Goodnight, Irene,* by Leadbelly (who, you'll remember, died in 1949) and *Tzena, Tzena, Tzena,* an Israeli folk song. Their finest album is THE WEAVERS AT CARNEGIE HALL.

The Weavers were all right. So are Peter, Paul, and Mary. As for the others—not to my taste.

8 The Lore and the Lure

Folk is part of popular commercial music. Millions of people listen, play guitars and sing, and, in one way or another, provide income for songwriters, professional performers, and assorted businessmen.

Big-scale profit making from folk songs is a relatively new thing, although investments were made as long as centuries ago. With folk songs the present owes much to the past.

Many songs still heard in America are traditional ones first sung by English, French, Irish, Negro, Scandinavian, Scotch, and Spanish immigrants. These songs, reflecting in bright and variegated strands the patterns of earlier times, have been rediscovered recently and used to enrich the present. Songs—made up or reworked by amateurs and semiprofessionals and passed around to neighbors and from generation to generation within a family—

have been collected by folklorists and compiled in collections or put on tapes and records. Picked up by an ever-growing number of professionals, these songs are then spread throughout the country and, in some cases, the world.

We have considered many examples of how singers and songwriters have made use of the past, and, at the same time, have kept up with the present. Singers' popularity, however, depends on more than themselves. It is also made possible by impresarios who promote concerts, who run clubs, and who bring imagination and zest to publicizing colorful talents; and, finally, it is made possible by critics, reporters, and disc jockeys who give the public a chance to find out what is happening.

This chapter is mostly about some of the men, both living and dead, who although not musicians in most cases have been or still are partly responsible for the current enthusiasm for folk singing.

As long ago as the late eighteen-hundreds Francis J. Child, the son of a Boston sailmaker, became a Harvard professor and published in five volumes THE ENGLISH AND SCOTTISH POPULAR BALLADS. It is *the* basic songbook, classifying and numbering as it does, 305 ballads—for example, *Lord Randall* (No. 12), *Sir Patrick Spens* (No. 58), and *Geordie* (No. 209). Child's work is available in a paperback edition published by Dover Publications.

Two decades later, Cecil Sharp, a professor from England, did for American ballads, especially those of the Appalachians, what Child had done for those of Great Britain.

Meanwhile, John Lomax, a Harvard scholar, traveled by train, on horseback, and sometimes on foot through the states west of the Mississippi River looking for folk songs. From that search came two books, COWBOY SONGS AND OTHER FRONTIER BALLADS (1910) and SONGS OF THE CATTLE TRAIL AND COW CAMP (1917). In 1933 John Lomax and his son Alan visited Negro convict camps in Texas, Louisiana, Mississippi, and Tennessee, as well as cotton

This pensive gentleman is Francis J. Child, a Harvard professor of the nineteenth century who compiled a catalog of English and Scottish ballads—a major songbook still referred to. He was among the first of many dedicated scholars in the field.

plantations and lumber camps, in search of Negroes who sang songs peculiar to the southern Negro way of life. The following year the Lomaxes included the best of these songs in another book, AMERICAN BALLADS AND FOLK SONGS. Here are a few of the songs in the collection: *John Henry, Casey Jones, The Hammer Song, Stewball, Stagolee, Railroad Bill, Sugar Babe, Little Brown Jug, Honey, Take a Whiff on Me, Go Way from My Window, Shorty George, Pick a Bale o' Cotton, Shortenin' Bread, Old Dan Tucker, Skip to My Lou, Git Along Little Dogies, Wicked Polly.*

Besides spending part of his youth traveling around the South recording folk songs in their natural settings for the Library of Congress, Alan Lomax is himself the author of several books, including MISTER JELLY ROLL, a re-creation and interpretation of Ferdinand Morton's life, and THE FOLK SONGS OF NORTH AMERICA IN THE ENGLISH LANGUAGE, an annotated songbook. Alan, whom Pete Seeger calls "the most important single figure" in folk music, is at work on a book about the relationship of music to social behavior in some three hundred of the world's cultures.

Two others eminent in the folk-music field are Carl Sandburg, who began playing the guitar at the turn of the century and who in the twenties compiled AMERICAN SONGBAG, and John Jacob Niles, a country-music researcher and musician with credits that include the songs *Venezuela* and *I Wonder As I Wander*.

To this group of men who have had a profound effect on the current interest in folk music must be added Moses Asch, founder in 1948 of Folkways Records. He and the late Marian Distler began the company with records of Cuban and American Indian music, American square dances, and jazz. Later, they added a series of records for children, an ethnic series, and various spoken-word, sound-effects, and science records.

Moe is also copublisher of Oak Publications and *Sing Out!* magazine. The record and publishing companies are located at 165 West 46th Street, New York, N.Y. 10036. In September, 1965,

Alan Lomax (left) has been described as "the most important single figure" in folk music by Pete Seeger (right). Along with his father, John Lomax— a Harvard scholar—Alan as a young man discovered, recorded, and encouraged many indigent back-country folk singers. He has continued to be active, especially through the Newport Folk Foundation.

Moe Asch announced the creation of a new record label, Verve/ Folkways (Verve is a subsidiary of MGM), to issue under his personal supervision a number of new records for mass distribution. At the same time, he assured his loyal followers that Folkways would continue to maintain its own extensive catalog of more than 1,200 LPs and would issue new records of its own for its specialized market. On the latter point he said:

"I want to reiterate right now, once and for all, that the cardinal concept in my life and work in relation to folk music and to records (and now in the publishing field) is that any documentation of the world has continuing validity as issued and produced—and will not be discontinued."

A heavyset formidable-looking man, Moe is said to have a mercurial temper and an unorthodox business philosophy—the latter evident from his practice of having recorded the greats of folk music when they were still unknown hoboes, street singers, wandering minstrels, hill people, and so forth. Artists he's recorded include Pete Seeger, Clarence Ashley, Big Bill Broonzy, Jack Elliott, John Greenway, Woody Guthrie, Lightnin' Hopkins, Cisco Houston, Blind Lemon Jefferson, Leadbelly, Sonny Terry, and Big Joe Williams.

According to the most ardent Moe Asch admirers, there wouldn't have been a modern folk-music boom if he hadn't issued the six-volume ANTHOLOGY OF AMERICAN FOLK MUSIC, which was produced and annotated by Harry Smith. It is said that no other source can compare as a learning place for young singers, now that there are few authentic street singers and hillbillies left.

The importance of records to the performance and appreciation of folk singing can't be overstressed. The white hillbilly and Negro country music sought out and recorded in the South in the twenties later became the source of many popular hits which swept around the nation and the world as a result of a major technological breakthrough.

Formally attired, as befits a gentleman of the old school, John Jacob Niles, in a high-tenor voice and to the accompaniment of the dulcimer, vigorously performs both his own and traditional folk songs. He has been active since World War I.

In the late forties, records made of vinyl (which never need wear out and can't be broken by accident) were put on the market. The new records were pressed from masters with grooves cut so closely together that a ten-inch disc provided twenty minutes of sound if revolved at thirty-three and one-third revolutions per minute. Swift changes with widespread consequences followed. Long-playing records, packaged in cardboard envelopes called "albums," grew from ten to twelve inches in diameter, while seven-inch discs, designed for forty-five revolutions per minute, were put on the market for both home phonographs and jukeboxes. A sleepy audio-equipment industry grew to giant size. All manner of components were developed and manufactured to record and reproduce sounds almost absolutely faithful to the original.

Hi-Fi became a household word, and phonograph records became big enough sellers to find a place even in the supermarket, where Van Cliburn's and Elvis' were sold side by side. Importantly, the record and radio businesses interacted so that both boomed. In the fifties, independent radio stations sprang up all over the nation. Most stations broadcast recorded music almost exclusively. Listeners heard the records and bought them. Sales and profits were handsome; more records were made; more were broadcast; and so on in an upward spiral.

Many small entrepreneurs tried to profit from the boom, but almost all failed. This is because pop-music records—including, after 1955, rock 'n' roll—take lots of money for promotion, and since nobody knows in advance what will sell, record companies issue songs by hundreds of artists to get one star who catches on and lasts. Either millions of dollars or a fantastic streak of luck is necessary. The big companies don't have to depend on luck. Those little companies (called "independents") which tried to find a place by recording jazz—which the big companies weren't much interested in—mostly went under. Americans, in spite of all the hoopla, have seldom shelled out to support jazz. Not only record companies with jazz policies but nightclubs, too, had trouble. The situation was about the same with folk music. Through the forties and into the fifties, few knew of it and fewer cared.

One who did, of course, was Moe Asch. Others who followed him, bringing a determination to create hi-fidelity recordings (not always achieved by Folkways) as well as profits, include the Solomon brothers of Vanguard and Jac Holzman of Elektra (both companies, or their subdivisions, record classical music too). The crowning glories of Vanguard's folk repertory are Joan Baez and the Newport Folk Festival albums. Elektra's current claim to serious attention rests on Phil Ochs and Tom Paxton and on the four LPs of the FOLK BOX—according to advertisements for it, the latter encompasses eighty-three folk songs and ballads representing jewels in the combined wealth of both Elektra and Folkways. It's a notable joint venture, but, unfortunately, the not-so-good is covered as well as the very good. The box would be twice as valuable if it held half the contents.

For the labels of all the companies, both big and small, that sell records in the folk field (including hillbilly and rock 'n' roll) see the long-playing record guide published monthly by W. Schwann. It's sold in record stores.

Others who do not function professionally either as singers or songwriters, but who are nevertheless important to folk music, are talent managers, concert promoters, critics, and club owners.

In the first category are Albert Grossman (Peter, Paul, and Mary; Bob Dylan), Manny Greenhill (Joan Baez; Flatt and Scruggs), and Harold Leventhal (Pete Seeger; Theodore Bikel), to name but a few of the singers handled by but a few of the managers.

Among promoters there is George Wein, who is one of those responsible for the Newport Folk Festivals.

Some of the more active critics and journalists are Robert Shelton of *The New York Times,* Ralph Gleason of the San Francisco *Chronicle,* Pete Welding of *Down Beat,* Irwin Silber, editor of *Sing Out!,* and Paul Nelson and Jon Pankake, editors of the *Little Sandy Review.*

As for club owners, they are a courageous lot, opening clubs as they do fully aware that the mortality rate is extremely high. Sometimes they can't make a go of it because the customers either don't show up often enough or don't spend enough when they do; sometimes because the rooms they can afford to rent are in buildings that have a remarkable proclivity for being pulled down to make way for newer, higher, more expensive structures; sometimes because of harassment. An example of the latter cast

Moses Asch has spent a good part of his working life recording folk songs and publishing books and a magazine about them and their performers. Now and for a long time to come listeners are and will be greatly indebted.

Albert Grossman, the most successful businessman in the folk field, operated the now defunct Gate of Horn club in Chicago in the nineteen-fifties and made his fortune in New York in the sixties managing Bob Dylan and Peter, Paul, and Mary.

its shadow at the end of 1965 over Clarence Hood, owner of the Gaslight Cafe on MacDougal Street. He did manage to satisfy the commands of city authorities to improve the building's facilities and the Gaslight did survive, but for a while it was touch and go.

An example of a coffeehouse fatality due to too many under-paying listeners was The Centaur in Chicago's Old Town. It was closed on Halloween, 1965—a ghostly event. Now, John Brown devotes himself to running his leather shop—sandals, pocket-books, crazy capes, and the like.

Old Town, by the way, is a mecca for hipsters, folk-song singers and listeners, teenyboppers and bagel bunnies, and conventioneers and their wives. Just four years ago it was a sleepy, forgotten part of Chicago. Now Old Town is Boom Town: on weekend nights the sidewalks of Wells Street—the MacDougal Street of the Midwest—are as crowded as those of Provincetown, Massachusetts, on the Fourth of July. For folk-singing enthusiasts twenty-one—the minimum legal drinking age in Illinois—or older the action is at Mother Blue's, where José Feliciano, the guitarist and singer, captivated Chicagoans before he achieved nationwide fame; Big John's, where the bands of Little Walter, Muddy Waters, and Paul Butterfield frequently play, and Poor Richard's, a former synagogue on the fringe of Old Town which now serves as a talking and drinking spot for such professionals as the bearded but bald-headed Shel Silverstein, creator of *Hey Nellie, Nellie* and *The Hills of Shiloh.*

One of the more successful midwest clubs is It's Here, in the north country of Chicago. Owned by Ed Gunger, it has been running to largely full capacity crowds for seven years. Six nights a week high school and college students pack in to sit and sprawl on cushions, to drink coffee and sodas, and, up to the fall of 1965, to listen to the Dayjobbers—Dave Brian and Jim Boyles, two guitarists and folk singers—who since have been appearing in spirits-serving establishments.

Meanwhile, back in Manhattan, where just about every entertainer hopes to end up, Israel Young holds forth: the Sage of Sixth Avenue. He's not easily pinned down, although I suppose he could be accurately called a folklorist, a discoverer (he set up Bob Dylan's first New York City concert), and an all-around stimulator.

Most important, Izzy runs the Folklore Center in Greenwich Village, now a wood-paneled, book-lined room-and-a-half on the second floor at 321 Sixth Avenue. The center is exactly that: a focal point where performers and enthusiasts wander in at all hours of the afternoon and evening to chat, to read the bulletin board, even occasionally to buy records or pamphlets or books.

To get a feeling for the magnetic attraction of 321 Sixth Avenue, consider the scene at 11 A.M., November 23, 1965. In the kitchen of Izzy's tiny, three-room apartment, two flights above the center, Big Joe Williams was in the midst of preparing a second batch of southern fried chicken, rice, and espresso coffee for Izzy, himself, and any fans or musicians who happened in. The

Not a singer, songwriter, or promoter, Israel Young has a huge, if immeasurable, influence upon both performers and their audiences. For over a decade he has observed, commented upon, and at times directed folk-singing trends from his base in Greenwich Village's Folklore Center.

extemporaneous breakfast developed because Big Joe had just arrived from Chicago—where he had been performing his blues at the Yellow Unicorn—to take part in a four-day blues session conducted by Izzy at the Cafe Au Go Go on Bleecker Street.

Izzy, who opened the center in 1957 after he quit being a premed student, became a public personality when he championed the cause of folk singing in Washington Square Park. The cause, which at times turned into a battle, set a precedent in seeking the right to sing in a public place. It was one of the few instances, at that time, when folk singers made history instead of just singing about it.

Trouble began in March, 1961, when the New York City Commissioner of Parks banned folk singing in the Square—an activity that had taken place there on warm Sunday afternoons since World War II. The commissioner had two excuses: (1) He wanted to rid the park of unsavory characters; (2) He wanted the grass to grow (even though the folk singing occurred by the fountain, which was often dry, and its surrounding acre of macadam). The commissioner never troubled to be rational; therefore, it is difficult to say what his real reason was, but being a bureaucrat with autocratic tastes, it is probable that he thought folk singing undignified.

Regardless of the reason for the ban, Easter Sunday was sad and lonely with no folk singing.

Izzy was disturbed, so the following day he met with the commissioner. He left disappointed and called upon folk singers and their friends to rally in the Square the following Sunday.

They did. Thousands of them. Izzy called for an orderly demonstration and addressed the crowd from the fountain. "We have no organization, no leaders. We have been singing here for seventeen years and never had any trouble. We have a right to sing here."

Just what the demonstrators thought, too. They began singing *We Shall Not Be Moved.* But moved they were when the riot squad arrived swinging clubs and arrested ten people. The Square was silenced, but the controversy grew.

RIGHT: *It was Izzy who led the protest against a ban on the folk singing in Washington Square in 1961.*

Folk singing in Washington Square became front-page news, with most of the newspapers backing law and order.

PARK SONGFEST
BOILS INTO RIOT
COPS ENFORCE BAN IN VILLAGE

—New York *Daily News*

3000 BEATNIKS
RIOT IN VILLAGE

—New York *Mirror*

Two days after the arrests, the commissioner began to lose his nerve. He said, "My order still stands and will continue to stand unless I am convinced beyond question of doubt that my judgment is wrong. I think I am right. At this point I have no intention of changing my mind. I will talk to the Mayor about this matter if the Mayor wants to talk about it."

The Mayor did. He backed up his commissioner, but not for long.

On April 12, Izzy, with the help of the American Civil Liberties Union, filed a petition asking the Supreme Court of the State of New York to direct the commissioner to issue a permit for folk singing in the Square.

The following Sunday, about five hundred folk singers, at the invitation of the Reverend Howard Moody, gathered in Judson Memorial Church, just outside the park, to sing. The police patrolled the park and kept it silent. On April 23, the very next Sunday, two thousand protesters jammed a street near the Square to poke fun at the commissioner. Mounted policemen stood by; on the next Sunday, a small but determined band of folk singers sat silently, for the most part, in the park; then one of their number was roughly arrested by two policemen; another riot almost occurred.

Early in May the court turned down Izzy's petition; so Izzy appealed—to the President, to the Governor, to the Attorney General—all to no avail. He also appealed to a higher court.

Meanwhile, the commissioner and the Mayor capitulated. They let the folk singers back, but to save face they cut the singing time from four to three hours on Sunday afternoon.

Izzy wasn't satisfied. He continued the struggle in court, and on July 6—some three months after the imbroglio began—the Appellate Division of the Supreme Court ruled that the commissioner acted improperly in refusing to permit the folk singing.

The commissioner said, "I never had the slightest hostility toward folk singing or folk singers. I'm a singer myself."

Izzy said, "I'm very glad justice has prevailed finally. I hope the commissioner will come down to the park and lead us in some songs."

Sad, but he never did.

Izzy, who, as much as anyone in the last decade had a hand in pushing folk singing forward, had been calling, for some time, for expansion of the term to include not only traditional songs (or new songs in old forms) but really new ones that interpret what's happening in our time.

In 1965 his call was answered as one folk singer after another, mostly following Bob Dylan's lead, put down the traditional guitar to pick up the sleek, free-form instruments made by Fender and Rickenbacker and plugged into gigantic amplifiers and speakers. It seems certain that within the next few years these small, folk-rock groups will grow into big bands with french horns, saxophones, and flutes, and that the melodies they play will move toward the complexity of jazz. Thus, an already stimulating bleep-bloop sound—combined with important message songs presented in the tradition of age-old ballads and blues—promises to get even more exciting.

Although folk singing has undergone a radical transformation with the advent of the electric guitar and the formation of folk-rock groups, the tradition of old-style, intensely personal, solo performances continues. For example, eighteen-year-old Arlo Guthrie (shown accompanying himself on an acoustical guitar at Poor Richard's during the winter of 1966) sings songs not only of his generation but also of his father's.

As with all things: the present comes from the past and leads to the future. By examining folk singing from the broadest possible view, by touching on highlights of citybilly, hillbilly, and rock 'n' roll, and by reviewing many popular performers of the past and profiling many of the present, we have established a guide for understanding the old and the new. Now, in order to partake you have to participate. Believe me, it's no struggle.

The following section not only lists all the records mentioned in this book but points out those I find most rewarding. I hope they entertain and enlighten you too.

Good listening.

ℰℤ List of Records

All the long-playing records mentioned in this book are listed here; a star appears before those I especially like. At the time of the book's publication, most of the records were available for sale in record shops or from the company whose name they bear.

ℰ𝒵 Index

PICTURE CREDITS: *John M. Bell, 113; Capitol Records, 105; The Chicago Sun-Times, 124; John Cohen (print courtesy Israel Young, The Folklore Center), 99; Columbia Records, 15, 96; Culver Pictures, 90; Diana J. Davies (from Nancy Palmer Agency), 38, 116; Decca Records, 57; Elektra Records, 18, 79 (top), 88; Folkways Records, 35, 43; David Gahr, 47, 64–65, 83, 119, 121; Jim Marshall, 2–3, 8, 11, 12, 21, 23, 24, 30, 70, 71, 72, 78 (top), 78 (bottom), 81, 84, 86, 102–103, 111, 117; New York Public Library, 110; RCA Victor Records, 79 (bottom); Steve Somerstein, 60; United Artists Corp., 74–75; United Press International, 52–53, 55; Vanguard Records, 49; Wide World Photos, 26–27, 67. Picture research by Patricia Crum.*